USEFUL
DELUSIONS

ALSO BY SHANKAR VEDANTAM

The Hidden Brain:
How Our Unconscious Minds Elect Presidents,
Control Markets, Wage Wars, and Save Our Lives

ALSO BY BILL MESLER

A Brief History of Creation:
Science and the Search for the Origin of Life (coauthor)

USEFUL DELUSIONS

The Power and Paradox
of the Self-Deceiving Brain

Shankar Vedantam
and Bill Mesler

W. W. NORTON & COMPANY
Independent Publishers Since 1923

The Poems of Emily Dickinson: Reading Edition, edited by Ralph W. Franklin, Cambridge, Mass.: The Belknap Press of Harvard University Press, Copyright © 1998, 1999 by the President and Fellows of Harvard College. Copyright © 1951, 1955 by the President and Fellows of Harvard College. Copyright © renewed 1979, 1983 by the President and Fellows of Harvard College. Copyright © 1914, 1918, 1919, 1924, 1929, 1930, 1932, 1935, 1937, 1942 by Martha Dickinson Bianchi. Copyright © 1952, 1957, 1958, 1963, 1965 by Mary L. Hampson.

For information about permission to reproduce selections from this book, write to Permissions, W. W. Norton & Company, Inc., 500 Fifth Avenue, New York, NY 10110

For information about special discounts for bulk purchases, please contact W. W. Norton Special Sales at specialsales@wwnorton.com or 800-233-4830

Manufacturing by Lakeside Book Company
Book design by Ellen Cipriano
Production manager: Anna Oler

Library of Congress Cataloging-in-Publication Data

Names: Vedantam, Shankar, author. | Mesler, Bill, author.
Title: Useful delusions : the power and paradox of the self-deceiving brain / Shankar Vedantam and Bill Mesler.
Description: First Edition. | New York : W. W. Norton & Company, 2021. | Includes bibliographical references and index.
Identifiers: LCCN 2020028515 | ISBN 9780393652208 (hardcover) | ISBN 9780393652215 (epub)
Subjects: LCSH: Deception. | Self-deception. | Truthfulness and falsehood. | Delusions.
Classification: LCC BF637.D42 V43 2021 | DDC 153.4—dc23
LC record available at https://lccn.loc.gov/2020028515

ISBN 978-1-324-02028-8 pbk.

W. W. Norton & Company, Inc., 500 Fifth Avenue, New York, N.Y. 10110
www.wwnorton.com

W. W. Norton & Company Ltd., 15 Carlisle Street, London W1D 3BS

1 2 3 4 5 6 7 8 9 0

To my mother, Vatsala, who showed me
that reality bends to willpower
—Shankar Vedantam

And to my mother, Chun Yun, a little girl from
Pyongyang, who survived wars and famines,
and willed herself across seas and continents

—Bill Mesler

For if people wish to believe a thing, and long for it and depend on it to be true, and feel the better for it, is it cheating to help them to their own belief . . . Is it not rather a charity, and a human kindness?

—MARGARET ATWOOD, *ALIAS GRACE*

Contents

Introduction

Shankar Vedantam

I n the winter of 2011, my wife, my daughter and I set out on a road trip from Washington, DC, to Toronto to visit some close friends. It was a beautiful drive that took us through the lush foothills of the Allegheny Mountain Range, and eventually past Lake Erie and Niagara Falls. But first we had to make a stop just outside of Pittsburgh, where I had an appointment with a felon.

The detour didn't surprise my family too much. We had made the drive before, and had stopped at a maximum security prison so I could interview a man convicted of murder for my book *The Hidden Brain*. This meeting was merely with a white-collar criminal. His old U.S. Marshall–issued "WANTED" poster noted that he was the founder of "a cult-type organization" called the "Church of Love." It would be more accurate to say he was a con artist who had managed to pull off one of the most bizarre and inventive scams in American history. His name was Donald Lowry.

Lowry first came to my attention some months earlier, as I

was reading an obscure academic paper. In passing, the paper mentioned some elements of Lowry's peculiar scheme, which it described, dryly, as a "rather inventive direct-mail program." I was intrigued and started to look for more information. Much to my surprise, there was a lot of it. If you are old enough to have read newspapers or watched television news in the late 1980s, you might have heard of the Church of Love. Lowry's case found its way into the *New York Times* and the *Los Angeles Times*, several national magazines, and the big four television networks. He was interviewed by Bill O'Reilly on *Inside Edition* and by Maury Povich on *A Current Affair*. His trial was covered by the Australian Broadcasting Corporation and by the magazine *Paris Match*, the largest newsweekly in France. His scam was the subject of an early and iconic episode of *Geraldo*.

The story was weird and captivating: A balding, middle-aged writer in a small Midwestern town had assumed the personas of dozens of fictitious women. He had written love letters in their voices to tens of thousands of men—the "inventive direct mail program." Each woman had her own unique writing style, vocabulary and backstory. The letters were printed *en masse*, but they featured numerous personal touches. Lowry used fonts that imitated actual handwriting, and the letters were often printed on paper tinted in delicate pastels. The notes featured girlish expostulations and whimsical digressions. Lots of men who received the love letters wrote back. In the course of weeks, months and sometimes years, they poured out their hearts to their fictitious correspondents. Many fell in love, and believed they had found their soulmates. They sent in hundreds of thousands of dollars to Lowry and his organization in order to keep the love letters coming. Some wrote wills bequeathing their estates to their imagined soulmates. Federal investigators eventually estimated that, by the end, Lowry's scheme had garnered millions of dollars. His business occupied the entirety of one of the most prominent downtown office buildings in Moline, Illinois, and he owned printing presses large enough to publish a medium-sized newspaper. His organization had fifty employees. By the time Lowry was arrested, he owned a fleet of twenty automobiles, including Rolls-Royces and Jaguars. He had a full-time personal mechanic.

I've always been intrigued by stories about con artists. Like art forgers, these criminals tend to be colorful, and their outlandish tales usually make for interesting journalism. But there was something about this case that struck me as completely unbelievable: When Lowry's scheme was unmasked, and he was brought to trial on charges of mail fraud in 1988, members of his love letter subscription service came to a courthouse in Peoria, Illinois—*to defend him.* Some testified that the "Church of Love" had kept them from addiction and loneliness—two members said the love letters had saved them from suicide. One man railed against the investigators who were trying to protect victims like himself. "The Postal Inspector ruined my life," he said.

What on earth was going on? Once the con was revealed, *why would the marks show up to defend the con artist?* It was as though deceiver and deceived were in it together, bound by a pact of complicity. I began discussing this strange story with science writer Bill Mesler. Our conversation provided the seeds for this book. (Although told in my voice and from my vantage point, the book that follows is the product of our collaboration.)

What began as curiosity morphed into a quest to understand the power—and paradox—of self-deception. It eventually led me to challenge fundamental aspects of my worldview. Somewhere along this journey, I realized that I had spent much of my adult life working on the subjects of delusion and self-deception. My book *The*

Hidden Brain, which eventually led to the *Hidden Brain* podcast and radio show, is all about peeling back the layers of lies that keep us from seeing reality clearly and from becoming our best selves. The virtue of uncovering mental errors and biases seem self-evident. We live in times that showcase the terrible effects of lies, scams and self-deception. Surely, all of us want to separate what is true from what is untrue. From Socrates on—*know thyself!*—philosophers and scientists have told us the highest good is to see things clearly, to tell delusion from reality. "The truth will set you free!" has long been the rallying cry of reformers and revolutionaries. How then to understand the members of Don Lowry's love-letter subscription scheme, who not only fell for an outlandish deception, but fought to preserve it when it was revealed to be a hoax?

The simplest answer to that question was the one showcased on *Geraldo* and by the media hordes that covered the case: Lowry's victims were poor, pathetic rubes. They were too weak to stand up for themselves when they discovered they had been taken for a ride. In one episode of his show, Fox impresario Geraldo Rivera brought in a member of the Church of Love, a model who worked for Lowry, and an assistant writer who helped with the letters. Rivera had plenty of props, including a negligee and a pair of lace panties, which he waved around energetically like flags. He described an "elaborate hoax."

Rivera held up one of the love letters that had been mailed to members. He read from it in a mock-seductive voice: *It somehow seems I've been living just for this moment. Your kisses were passionate, but not demanding, threatening. I lay down on the sofa and you lay beside me, almost on top of me. The rain beat a rhythmic tattoo on the roof. The wind whistled overhead. It was a night made for love. It was a night made for us.*

The camera panned to Carl Cornell, an eighty-four-year-old

Arkansas man who was a long-standing member of the Church of Love. It was Cornell's birthday, Rivera noted, and the trip to the studio in New York was his first on an airplane. Cornell listened patiently as Geraldo disparaged the love-letter scheme. When he finally got a chance to speak, his eyes flashed anger: "You paid my fare up here. If I'd have known it'd be this kinda show, I wouldn'ta come."

Geraldo tried to placate him, but Cornell would have none of it: "I came up here to tell you the truth, and I'm not getting a chance to tell the truth."

"Carl, I don't want to hurt your feelings, I'm talking about facts," Rivera said.

"You're not hurting my feelings," Cornell responded. "You're hurting my friends."

When I first stumbled on the story of the Church of Love, I subscribed to the conventional explanation that Lowry was a clever con artist, and that his victims were gullible fools. But after interviewing members of the Church of Love and reading their testimonies at Lowry's trial, after interviewing Lowry himself during that 2011 trip, and after reading hundreds of research papers in medicine, psychology and economics, I came to doubt the conventional narrative. For one thing, I began to see that the self-deception of the members, their *complicity* in Lowry's scheme, was far from an aberration. Similar examples abounded. Most were less dramatic. Many were clothed in respectability—no one would go around calling them "scams" or demand they be prosecuted in the courts. All involved dances of complicity between deceivers and deceived. These pacts of deception and self-deception were sometimes explicit but, far more often, implicit and unspoken.

The ubiquity of these examples prompted me to revisit another fundamental assumption: Was it possible, I asked myself, that for at least some members, the Church of Love *had* provided a valuable service? That couldn't be the case, could it? The whole thing was a hoax. But what then to make of members who said the love letters had saved their lives, or kept them from addiction and suicide? A disturbing question popped into my head: Could self-deception ever lead to *good* outcomes? Again, the moment I asked this question, I began to see plenty of examples. I realized that one reason people cling to false beliefs is because *self-deception can sometimes be functional*—it enables us to accomplish useful social, psychological or biological goals. Holding false beliefs is not always the mark of idiocy, pathology or villainy.

As I started to question my assumptions, I began to see cracks in the façade of the Temple of Rationality. I saw that pacts of complicity between deceivers and self-deceivers are not only ubiquitous, but often useful, regularly functional and sometimes essential. They can shape the quality of our relationships. They can underpin the success of our groups. They can even predict how long we'll live.

Believing what we want to believe and seeing what we want to see, I slowly came to understand, is less a state of mind, or a reflection of one's intelligence, and more a response to one's circumstances. Foregoing self-deception isn't merely a mark of education or enlightenment—it is a sign of *privilege*. If you don't believe in Santa Claus or the Virgin Birth, it's because your life does not depend on your believing such things. Your material, cultural and social worlds are providing you with other safety nets for your psychological and physical needs. But should your circumstances change for the worse, were the pillars of your life to buckle and sway, your mind, too, would prove fertile ground for the wildest self-deceptions. There are, as we say, no atheists in foxholes.

. . .

At the core of our troubled relationship with the truth lies a dilemma: We need hope in order to function, but the world gives us endless reasons not to be hopeful. For most people on the planet, to forswear self-deception is to invite despair and dysfunction. This is especially clear when you step back and look at the big picture: If all life on earth was mapped on a timeline that stretched one hundred yards in length, humans arrived on the scene an eighth of an inch from the very end. All of human history—the rise and fall of every empire, every score of music and every book ever written, all the vast encyclopedias of human knowledge—everything falls into that last tiny sliver. If you step back even further, and look not just at life on earth but at our planet itself, human beings vanish into insignificance: Earth is one of a hundred billion planets, and that's just in our galaxy. That galaxy is one of two trillion galaxies. Humans are a tiny part of a very big universe. Our own existence as individuals? That's even more fragile, by many orders of magnitude.

How does this make you feel? Understanding something about the scale of time and space can produce wonder. But awareness of our own insignificance can also be a source of deep terror and dejection. In the very near future lie irrelevance, oblivion and erasure. If we were to speak truthfully, each of our lives is trivial, unimportant and easily forgotten.

This is not a useful attitude when it comes to ensuring our survival and the survival of our genes. If we are to roll the Sisyphean boulder up and down the hill, as required for our survival and the well-being of our progeny, it isn't helpful to feel our lives are useless or unimportant. This is why, in every culture around the world, people reach for beliefs that tell them that their lives have purpose and meaning. Nations and tribes convince us that, by becoming part of large groups, we can transcend our own brief existence as individuals. Nearly every religion in the world offers reassurances about what happens to you after you die. Poking holes in these claims is easy, because they are often illogical and far-fetched. Books such as *The God Delusion* by Richard Dawkins advise us to peer fearlessly into the void, to accept our irrelevance with good cheer. But this belies the real challenge: Most people without endowed professorships at Oxford University find it difficult to think of their own unimportance with equanimity. In fact, in a meeting at his beautiful home at Oxford some years ago, I asked Dawkins this question: Separate from whether the claims made by religions are true, should a person experiencing great suffering, but who feels their life is made bearable by a religious belief in the afterlife, be stripped of the comfort of their convictions? Dawkins was silent. If you're the kind of person who believes people with terminal illnesses should be stripped of their illusions about a heavenly afterlife, you sound the way I sounded in my twenties. Fine. But remember this: If self-deception is *functional*, then it will endure, regardless of all the best sellers that criticize it. Life, like evolution and natural selection, ultimately doesn't care about what's true. *It cares about what works.*

Consider this simplest of examples—the organ you are using to read this book: In any given second, the human eye collects about a billion bits of information. This flood of data is compressed a thousand times, and only one million bits of information are sent to the brain via the optic nerve. The brain keeps just forty bits of this data, and discards the rest. As the cognitive psychologist and author Donald Hoffman explains, this is like taking an actual book, compressing the chapters into Cliffs Notes, then taking those notes and throwing away nearly everything until you are left with a blurb.

The amazing thing is not that your brain reduces books to

blurbs on a moment-to-moment basis: It is that your brain gives you the *illusion* that you are seeing everything, that you are taking in the whole book. An engineer might say that what has unfolded is a profound delusion—what we think we see bears almost no resemblance to reality. But most of us would say that, subjectively, it feels, well, normal. It turns out there are excellent reasons for your eyes and brain to do all this filtering. Indeed, to see reality clearly would leave us worse off, not better. Our eyes and brain are not in the truth business; they are in the functionality business, and it turns out that discarding nine hundred and ninety-nine million, nine hundred and ninety-nine thousand, nine hundred and sixty bits of data out of every billion is extremely functional.

What happens with visual information also happens in nearly every part of our mental lives. We think we are seeing, hearing and processing the truth, but we often are not. As with our eyes, it turns out there are excellent reasons to prioritize functionality over reality in every domain. Yes, this means you miss the truth, but it gets you to the real goal: Your brain has been designed to help you survive, to forage for opportunities, to get along with mates and friends, to raise offspring to adulthood, and to avoid feelings of existential despair. From the perspective of evolution, objective truth is not only not the goal, it is not even the only path to the goal.

Sigmund Freud once compared the mind to the city of Rome. Like the actual city, he said, the mind has layers, each built atop the last. Many of Freud's notions have been discredited by empirical neuroscience and psychology, but there is a great truth in this elegant idea. As the product of a lengthy process of evolution, the *faculties* of our brains have emerged layer by layer over millions of years. Some faculties are virtually brand new. Others are ancient. Circuits in our brains that produce the emotion of fear, for example, are very similar to brain circuits that regulate fear in species that evolved millions of years before humans did. Our brains duplicate—or *conserve*—systems that helped our evolutionary ancestors survive. The mental faculties that were the last to evolve—the newest buildings in this very old city—do things that are inconceivable for other species. We can anticipate and imagine what will happen far into the future. We can carry out plans whose outcomes won't be seen for decades. We are unrivaled in our capacity to exercise reason and logic. For example, when our scientific instruments show us that reality is not as it seems—that an earth that looks flat is actually spherical—we have the capacity to overrule what *feels true* in favor of what *we know to be true*. These newest mental abilities make us proud—and they should. They are responsible for the achievements of science and technology; they have helped us form self-regulating political systems of great stability; they are the lifeblood of art and philosophy.

But the brilliance of our newest mental faculties has caused many intelligent people to believe a startling untruth—that logic and rationality are *all that matter*. Many of us—and I long counted myself among this group—believe that the world would be a better place if we could simply use reason and rationality to solve every problem. What this worldview fails to comprehend, what *I* failed to comprehend, is that reason and logic might well be the pinnacle of our mental faculties, but they are only the newest settlements atop a much larger, ancient city. That older city, often invisible, remains. Not only is it still with us, it plays a vital role in many aspects of survival, reproduction and adaptation. The invisible city establishes the boundaries of what we see and what we fail to see. If reason and logic tell us how to play the game, the invisible city defines the rules of the game. It is the template, over which the skyscrapers of reason and rationality loom. The buried city of ancient Rome is the blueprint, the map, of modern Rome. Believing that reason and logic are all that matter is like imagining that a great city is only about its present, that the past does not matter and plays no role in shaping it.

This book argues that across many domains today, and especially where we see the forces of culture and reason and logic besieged by unreason, tribalism and prejudice, we are really seeing projections of a war raging inside our own heads. Conflicts between tradition and modernity have parallels inside the brain. When the skyscrapers of reason and rationality act as though *they are the entire city*, they invite rebellion. That's because human thriving is deeply reliant on the workings of the ancient brain. For all the contempt the rational brain might have for its irrational and illogical counterparts, the new and the old systems in the brain are inextricably yoked together. We can no more tear them apart and discard one of them than we can destroy sewer lines, power grids and water supplies and still expect a city to produce great plays and scientific discoveries.

If the forces of logic and rationality often seem ineffective at fighting superstition, delusion and conspiracy theories, it's because the "new city of Rome" speaks a different language than the "old city of Rome." The two cities have different value systems. They have different ways of knowing. When the rational brain claims to have all the answers, it often ends up being misunderstood, undermined or ignored. To create a world that produces the best in human beings, we must certainly be informed by reason, rationality and science, but we must also deploy the insights of logic using aspects of our minds that are prone to storytelling, symbols—and self-deception.

Lots of books have been written about the negative consequences of delusion and self-deception. Many of them are very good. Their authors are informed by the terrible downsides of self-deception. They see the catastrophic consequences of gullibility in politics, business and personal relationships. I share their concerns about the great costs exacted by deception and self-deception. My goal here is not to reject rationality—or to defend con artists, hucksters and liars—but to make the argument that just because self-deception can lead us to ruin, it does not necessarily follow that it has no role to play in ensuring our well-being. Just because reason and rationality can see clearly into the future does not mean that they alone can ensure human welfare.

Rather than seek to annihilate self-deception and all it represents, a better goal would be to think carefully about what it does, and ask ourselves how we can work with it. In other words, we ought to care less about whether something is simply true or untrue and ask more complicated questions: What are the consequences of self-deception? Whom does it serve? Do the benefits justify the costs?

At a minimum, I hope this book prompts you to acknowledge the great debt you owe to the many self-deceptions that sustain your life. Indeed, even if your goal is to fight self-deception, you cannot do it without first understanding its profound power. We are not just in a war with con artists, conspiracy theorists and demagogues. We are in a war with ourselves. Our minds are not designed to see the truth, but to show us selective slices of reality, and to prompt us toward predetermined goals. Even worse, they are designed to do all this while giving us the *illusion* that we are seeing reality. We can believe that we are thinking clearly, acting rationally and fighting for the truth, even as we are beguiled into seeing what is functional for our groups, our families and ourselves—and imagining it to be the truth. The four chapters that make up Part I of this book start with everyday examples of this idea. Part II includes an extended account of the Church of Love—it will serve as case study for the role that self-deception plays in our romantic lives and our search for meaning. Part III explores how pacts of deception and self-deception organize our communities, tribes and nations.

The psychological forces that made it difficult for the members of the Church of Love to see reality accurately fill all our lives. If we seem less credulous, it's only because circumstances have not tested us to the same extent. Put another way, those poor, pathetic rubes—but for a few strokes of luck—are us.

PART I

Everyday Life

1

Hot Air

*I am always saying "Glad to've met you" to somebody I'm not
at all glad I met. If you want to stay alive, you have to say that
stuff, though.*

J. D. Salinger, *The Catcher in the Rye*

Jorge Trevino is a professional liar. When we hear the word
"liar," the image that usually springs to mind is of a malevolent
schemer whispering lies, deceits and half-truths from the shadows, like Iago in William Shakespeare's *Othello*. Trevino is nothing like that. He is friendly and good-natured, one of the most
affable people you'd ever meet. He oozes emotional intelligence.
A lot of it is innate—he's always been a people person. But a lot
of it has been honed over thirty years working in the hospitality
industry.

A native of the Mexican border town of Matamoras, Trevino
started out doing odd jobs in the employee break room of the Ritz
Carlton in Houston, Texas. Over the years, he worked his way up to
management positions, including Director of Guest Services at the
Ritz Carlton in Laguna Beach, California. Eventually, he moved
on to the boutique hotel chain Kimpton and finally to Hyatt, where
he became Executive Vice President for Brand Operations. He

spends much of his time training employees in newly opened hotels around the world.

This often involves teaching prospective staff to do little things to make sure their customers feel cherished. "Sometimes," Trevino says, "this can be as simple as 'How are you?' in the hallway." It's about projecting warmth, sincerity and generosity, about being kind and friendly to people even when your own feelings might pull you in the opposite direction. Trevino calls this "the people thing"—the ability to make customers feel cared about no matter the circumstances, and no matter how you might really feel. Another word for it would be "deception."

Now, maybe a waiter really does have a special bond with a diner. Perhaps the flight steward really does think you are special. But even the friendliest people person can't maintain the level of "sincere friendliness" that someone in the service industry is expected to maintain all the time. "It's endless," says Trevino. "I don't think most people can understand how hard it is to be 'on' eight hours, ten hours, twelve hours a day."

To be good at one's job in the hospitality industry, Trevino says, employees need to project the same warmth to everyone, even the most unreasonable, angry customer. It's far from easy. "The expectations of the guests are huge, and they will attack," he says. Little tricks can help, such as making sure to always sit a hostile customer down. ("Standing," he explains, is "a very pugilistic pose.") But the most important thing is to always be polite, to exude empathy even when "you just want to punch them in the face and say 'get real.'"

One time, when Trevino was filling in as manager of the Ritz Carlton Houston during the 1992 Republican Convention, a man he describes as a "very large, angry Texan" grabbed him by the collar and tried to yank him across the front desk. (Trevino is five feet, seven inches tall.) "You just give them a chauffeur and a driver," he says. "And you tell them you are going to give them champagne and orange juice."

Looking back, Trevino can laugh about that incident. But another experience makes him choke back tears. It makes him "so angry, so hurt" just to dredge up the memory. It happened when he was Director of Guest Services at the Ritz Carlton, San Francisco. A couple from England was checking in, and the room they had been promised wasn't available. Trevino arranged for them to spend the night at the Fairmont, one of the best hotels in the city. "It was fairly early in the morning," he says. "I put them in the car, a van. I was sitting in the front passenger seat, saying, 'We're putting you up in one of the best hotels in the city.' Suddenly I felt spit on my neck. I remember looking for a Kleenex and wiping the back of my head. But the whole time I was apologizing to them and telling them how sorry I was. I made sure that they got an hour-and-a-half couples massage when they got back to the hotel the next day."

Psychologists and sociologists have long recognized how difficult it is to suppress one's natural emotions in such situations. They recognize that the McDonald's employee who takes your drive-thru order, the flight attendant dealing with angry travelers on a crowded plane, the deferential waiter who brings you umbrella drinks as you lounge by the pool, all are performing not just labor, but "emotional labor."

Most of us think of courteous customer service as a good thing. (It is.) What we fail to see is how it involves innumerable acts of deception on the part of providers and self-deception on the part of consumers. And customer service is only the professional version of what is expected of us all. We are taught to speak politely to each other, to proffer verbal lubrications that can ease the frictions of interpersonal contact. In kindergarten, children are told, "If you can't say something nice, don't say anything"—which is another way of telling Sarah to keep what she really thinks of Jeff to herself, and to allow Jeff to maintain his high opinion of himself. In marital therapy, psychologists tell squabbling couples to practice "slow starts" in conversation, which means that if you think your partner is being a jerk, you should say, "I want you to know how much I love and appreciate all you do, Trevor, but there are times when your behavior hurts my feelings." Harmony in many settings is largely a consequence of the ability of participants to cushion their disagreements in a pleasant haze of humor, flattery and kindness. *Tell me lies, tell me sweet little lies*, crooned the rock band Fleetwood Mac. When I was a kid, I remember reading about the importance of being polite: "Do you think blowing 'hot air' is unimportant?" the book asked. "Remember, when you drive in a car, it's a cushion of hot air in your tires that keeps you from feeling each bump in the road!"

Obviously, the professional courtesies of customer service and the hot air of interpersonal communication constitute minor lies. But these trivial acts of deception and self-deception contain the same psychological elements that appear in more serious forms of deceit. Studying them carefully helps us understand how the dance between those forces shapes our thinking and behavior. Guests at Trevino's hotels are invited to believe a fiction—that they are valued, appreciated and loved just for who they are. No matter how obnoxious and unpleasant they might be, no matter how rudely their kids behave, visitors at Trevino's hotels expect "service with a smile."

Trevino's customers expect not only the fiction of loving attention, but the fiction that such warmth is not being purchased for money. Many service industries go out of their way to hide the transactive nature of their relationship with customers. When I visited Disney World some years ago, the front-desk clerk sporting Mickey Mouse ears issued my family wristbands. They were called "MagicBands." If you wanted to buy something, all you had to do was to wave your hand like a magician. The bands were electronically linked to my credit card. In its promotional material, Disney doesn't explain that the wristbands are a way to silently transfer money from families to a multibillion-dollar corporation. It merely says, "MagicBands add a touch of magic to your vacation." Restaurants, especially fancy ones, rarely tell you how much your meal costs. The waiter doesn't come up to you after you eat and say, "OK, that will be eighty-seven dollars and fifty cents." The bill comes discreetly tucked away between the flaps of a leather "check-presenter." Ride-share apps like Uber and Lyft take these deceptions a step further—you can summon a cab, get a ride, and step out at your destination without once reaching for your purse or having any discussions about money.

In personal settings, the emotional labor needed to cushion the truth explains why long-married couples will tell you that marriage *is work*. Friends and colleagues sometimes fare better in their interactions than married couples because friends and colleagues usually go out of their way to avoid displeasing each other, or revealing sources of irritation. (The stakes of fighting, ironically, are actually higher between friends than between married couples: A single fight between friends can spell the end of a friendship.) People who wish to maintain friendships are generous in taking the other person's point of view, lavish with compliments and slow to criticism. Each of those things involves complicities of deception and self-deception.

When we think of lies, we tend to think of big lies, often those told by very important people. You can mark the passage of the last half century of American history with a list of such deceptions: Lyndon B. Johnson and the Gulf of Tonkin; Richard Nixon and Watergate; Bill Clinton's "I-did-not-have-sexual-relations-with-that-woman" television statement; Colin Powell's UN speech claiming the United States possessed incontrovertible proof of weapons of mass destruction in Iraq; Donald Trump's "birther" allegations about President Barack Obama.

But vastly more common are the lies and deceptions that we think of as social niceties. Our day-to-day conversations are filled with them. In a 1975 paper titled "Everybody Has to Lie," the sociologist Harvey Sacks, founder of a field called "conversation analysis," detailed the myriad deceptions found in ordinary, day-to-day settings, beginning with basic greetings, usually some version of "How are you?" in which the person who asks doesn't actually care, and the person who answers isn't expected to be truthful.

We say "Have a nice day" when we couldn't care less. We say "That was a lovely dinner" even when the meal was awful. "I'm so glad you could come" sometimes means "Thank God this interminable evening is finally over!" These lies are prescribed by the unwritten rules of social etiquette. Children who don't lie convincingly in social settings are later reproached by their parents. In many situations, Sacks found, lying is more common than telling the truth.

Imagine for a moment a world that did not have such daily deceptions. The left-hand column is what your Mondays might sound like with social niceties. The column on the right is what they would be like without "the cushion of hot air."

WHAT YOU SAY (THE "CUSHION" OF HOT AIR)	WHAT YOU THINK (AKA THE TRUTH)
Good morning, honey!	Where's my coffee?
(To your neighbor) Beautiful day!	God, I've forgotten his name again.
(In the elevator) Could you please push six for me?	SIX, goddammit!
A colleague: How was your weekend? You: Just wonderful.	I need more coffee before I can engage in meaningless chit-chat.
A colleague: I had the funniest dream. You: Really? What was it about?	God, not again!
Thanks so much for coming in.	You still work here?
(At lunch in the cafeteria) Join us, please.	Go away.
So sorry about that report.	If you knew what you wanted, and could communicate clearly, I wouldn't have needed to do this three times.
(To coworkers) Have a lovely evening!	I can't wait until I never see this place again.
(To your kid) It sounds like the test was really difficult, sweetheart.	If you had studied for this test, you wouldn't have gotten a C.
Good night, honey!	(Sullen, self-pitying silence)

In the sketch comedy *Key & Peele*, the actors Keegan-Michael Key and Jordan Peele had a recurring segment where one of them played the President Obama most of us saw on television—reserved, polite and courteous—while the other channeled Obama without his superhuman anger filter, an alter-ego named "Luther." At the 2015 White House Correspondents Dinner, the highlight for me was a sketch that the real President Obama pulled off with Keegan-Michael Key, in which Key voiced Obama's putatively unspoken thoughts.

> OBAMA: In our fast-changing world, traditions like the White House Correspondents' Dinner are important.
> LUTHER: I mean, really! What is this dinner? And why am I required to come to it?
> OBAMA: Because despite our differences, we count on the press to shed light on the most important issues of the day.
> LUTHER: And we can count on Fox News to terrify old white people with some nonsense!

One criticism that both Democrats and Republicans made of President Donald Trump is that he lacked a filter. If he thought Mexicans coming over the border were rapists, he said so. Of course, another term to describe such behavior is "candor." You knew where you stood when you spoke with The Donald, since he made his mind abundantly clear in a stream of tweets, insults and inflated claims. For a long time, Americans dreamed of getting a president who was "authentic." But throughout the Trump presidency, most Democrats, and large numbers of Republicans, wished they could install a filter between Trump's brain and his mouth. They wanted him to shut up about things he clearly believed were true.

Most conventional politicians are skilled at such deceptions. They modify their views to fit their audience's needs. Experiments show that this is also true for the rest of us. If you give people different facts and ask them to share the facts with an audience, people will select those messages that are most likely to match their audience's preexisting beliefs. Social psychologist E. Tory Higgins found that this dance of deception and self-deception—where speakers try to please audiences, and audiences appreciate speakers whose views match their own—comes with a special twist. After selectively choosing which messages to share, speakers come to believe that the facts they have communicated are indeed what they themselves actually believe. Higgins calls this "audience tuning." In other words, it isn't just that politicians tell us what we want to hear. By telling us what we want to hear, politicians come to think that *they believed those things all along*. It has been theorized that this tendency to believe our own lies—which in turn helps us lie more effectively—is the evolutionary origin of self-deception in human beings. (An organism that can deceive better would have an advantage over its competitors.) The psychological forces that "sync" a politician with her audience are strongest when there is a powerful bond between the two. Is all this irrational? Sure. But does it make sense from the point of view of our social and emotional goals? Absolutely. We evolved to be a social species, so it should not be surprising that we come hardwired to modulate our views in order to fit in with those around us, to get along with others.

The people most skilled at these sophisticated forms of deception often come across as charismatic, even "sincere." Think of how Ronald Reagan and Bill Clinton were received during their time in office and on the campaign trail. People around them felt special; they felt *liked*. We all know people like Reagan and Clinton in our lives. They appear interested in what we have to say. They ooze empathy, and they put us at ease. We have positive terms to describe such people—we call them "emotionally intelligent." Oddly, given how much we say we care about the truth, we don't have positive things to say about people who just say what is on their minds. We don't have a word for someone who doesn't lie *enough* when the rules of social engagement demand it. But we know such people when we see them. They come across as cold or cruel.

In William Shakespeare's great tragedy *King Lear*, an old king who is about to apportion his kingdom between his three daughters demands first to be told how much they love him. The older daughters, recognizing the game being played, tell Lear what he wants to hear.

> **GONERIL:**
> *Sir, I love you more than words can wield the matter;*
> *Dearer than eye-sight, space, and liberty;*
> *Beyond what can be valued, rich or rare;*
> *No less than life, with grace, health, beauty, honour;*
> *As much as child e'er loved, or father found;*
> *A love that makes breath poor, and speech unable;*
> *Beyond all manner of so much I love you.*

But the youngest daughter, Cordelia, finding such protestations distasteful, declines to produce the hot air her father demands.

> **CORDELIA:**
> *I love your majesty*
> *According to my bond, nor more nor less.*

Lear, furious, cuts Cordelia out of her inheritance. The older daughters promptly betray Lear once they have their hands on his kingdom. The moral of the story, Shakespeare suggests, is to be rational: Avoid mistaking showy love for actual love. That's all very well, but I would suggest a different truth: If we were stronger and wiser creatures—less Lear-like—you could simply tell us the truth and we would welcome it. But since we are vain and insecure, fearful and petty, fragile and weak, only a fool presents the unvarnished truth and expects to be properly heard. In this (as in many matters) I side with Emily Dickinson:

> Tell all the truth but tell it slant—
> Success in Circuit lies
> Too bright for our infirm Delight
> The Truth's superb surprise
> As Lightning to the Children eased
> With explanation kind
> The Truth must dazzle gradually
> Or every man be blind—

In recent years, researchers have empirically demonstrated what most of us know intuitively: Civility and "hot air" are essential to the functioning of teams and organizations. Rudeness in the workplace can impair how we think and act. In one experiment, volunteers asked to show up at a lab were greeted by a "professor" who told them that the meeting room had changed. Some volunteers were politely directed to another room. Others were told: "Can't you read? There is a sign on the door that tells you that the experiment will be in [a different room]. But you didn't even bother to look at the door, did you? Instead, you preferred to disturb me and ask for directions when you can clearly see that I am busy. I am not a secretary here, I am a busy professor." Volunteers spoken to rudely subsequently solved fewer anagram puzzles, and demonstrated less creativity when it came to thinking up different uses for a brick. They were also less helpful to others. Nearly three-quarters of the volunteers spoken to politely helped another person pick up dropped books without being asked. Of the volunteers spoken to rudely, not even a quarter offered unsolicited help.

At one of my first newspaper reporting jobs, an editor gathered all the young journalists one morning and imparted some wisdom: "No one," he said, "ever got fired for doing a bad job. People get fired for being assholes." That's not entirely true. I've seen people lose their jobs because of incompetence. But there is great truth in the advice. Human beings are a social species, and our brain systems keenly attune us to social niceties. Getting along with others is absolutely vital to our survival. If you run roughshod over other people's feelings and pride, saying you are speaking the truth—or defending reason—will not help you if the tide of public opinion turns against you.

This is why we teach our kids to say please and thank you, even when they can get what they want without being polite. We teach them to be kind and generous, even when they don't feel like it. We make them smile when guests come over, even if they can't stand those guests. We understand, intuitively and automatically, that some amount of deception is a necessary price to pay for entry into the human club. In turn, we expect such deception from others.

Our brains understand, through rules passed down across millions of years, that survival is a tough business and you don't want to make more enemies than you need. Politeness in human groups is mirrored by rules of conduct that govern other species. If you have ever seen millions of starlings coordinate their behavior, each bird flying wingtip to wingtip with the next, with sudden swerves wordlessly communicated across the entire flock, you understand how important social coordination has been through our long evolutionary history.

If you want to truly understand how reliant you are on lies to help you navigate your social world, just try to go a few days *without* lying. Unless you are incredibly socially inept—or just cruel—it's likely you can't. This was something University of California, Santa Barbara, psychologist Bella DePaulo found out in 1996 while conducting a study of lying. "I started out looking at nonverbal cues to deception," says DePaulo. "But as I kept doing the research and looking at the literature, it just astounded me that the most basic questions about deception had not been answered: namely how often we lie."

DePaulo's study was a "diary study" in which the subjects were simply asked to make note of the lies they told throughout the day. She found that most people tell about one lie per day. Subsequent studies suggest DePaulo's results were extremely conservative. Most people didn't count the small social lies—the lies of politeness—that Sacks analyzed. In a more recent study conducted by Robert Feldman, in which he filmed conversations between total strangers meeting for the first time, subjects admitted to lying about three times for every *ten minutes* of conversation—and some lied as many as twelve times. Despite the fact that DePaulo's findings were modest and, in hindsight, conservative, they were initially met with skepticism and disbelief. It is disquieting to think of ourselves as serial liars. Many of her students flat-out claimed they *never* lied. She had a simple response for them: She asked them to see how long they could go without lying. Most couldn't go more than a few days. "No one ever got through that assignment," she says. They discovered what DePaulo already knew, that "trying to be totally honest all the time was not really a good thing and probably not even possible."

One major problem the students encountered was a kind of lie they had not really thought about—one far more common than the nefarious deceptions the world talks about: "A lot of the lying is this lying because we don't want to hurt other people, or we want to go along with what they want to think and what they are feeling," she says. "It's a domain of kindness to those we care about. It's not that we don't value honesty, it's that we value something else more. The something else could be the other person's feelings, your feelings of loyalty toward them."

It should not be surprising, therefore, that we lie most regularly to those who are closest to us, to people whom we care about deeply. As DePaulo says, "Those caring lies, those kindhearted lies, are like gifts we give to the people we care about the most."

If the rational mind says, "speak the truth, no matter the consequences," more ancient algorithms in the brain whisper, "make sure you get along with others and tend to your relationships." The two systems speak different languages: One is explicit, the other is often implicit. One appeals to logic, the other to expedience. One cares deeply about the truth. The other cares deeply about outcomes.

2

Everything Is Going to Be OK

Nothing shows why
At this unique distance from isolation
It becomes still more difficult to find
Words at once true and kind,
Or not untrue and not unkind.

Philip Larkin, *Talking in Bed*

The German philosopher Immanuel Kant really hated lies. He went so far as to argue that we must tell the truth even when responding to a murderer asking about the whereabouts of an intended victim. "Truthfulness," Kant once wrote, "is a duty that must be regarded as the basis for all duties." While few would go so far as to tell a murderer where his future victim really is, most would agree with Kant's sentiment that lies are bad and that the truth is good. Honesty is one of our most cherished virtues. Polls show that Americans rank honesty as the most important factor they consider in choosing a president, above leadership or intelligence (although the results of some recent presidential elections suggest Americans may be deceiving themselves).

Yet for all our professed devotion to honesty, come Christmastime, the parents of most children in America will spend their days claiming that an obese man with a white beard and a red suit is going to slide down the chimney with presents. This is not one of the simple lies of social discourse that we discussed in the last chapter, but the next aspect of our story. These lies are pacts of deception and self-deception prompted by deep love and kindness.

When my daughter was four, she asked me a question out of the blue: "Is Rudolph the Red-nosed Reindeer real?" We were in the car and I was focused on the road. Without thinking, I gave her my professional opinion: "I don't think so, sweetheart." When I glanced at her in the rearview mirror, I knew I had made an error. Not a factual error, but a human error—an error in parenting. My daughter—who has always had a diplomatic way about her—had an expression on her face that told me she didn't like what I had said, but was formulating the right way to criticize it. (Clearly, she is more emotionally intelligent than I am.) Finally, after several minutes of squirming and fidgeting, she blurted out, "That's not true. Because if Rudolph isn't real, then who would pull Santa's sleigh?" I had the good sense at this point to say, "You know, I think you're absolutely right."

A wealth of social science studies show that parents spend more time trying to instill honesty in their children than any other single virtue. Yet research also tells us that lies are a widely used tool in parenting. Santa, it turns out, is just the start. Consider the story of George Washington and the cherry tree. You have almost certainly heard it many times: When America's future first president was just a lad, he chopped down his father's favorite cherry tree. When his father came home and found the beloved tree was dead, he was furious. He wanted to know who chopped it down. "I cannot tell a lie, Papa," young George replied. "I chopped down that tree." Rather than punish George for cutting down the tree, his father embraced him for being honest. The moral is that we should never lie, even when admitting the truth is difficult. But the story of George Washington and the cherry tree is itself a lie, the product of a parson of dubious character named Mason Weems who, in 1800, tried to cash in on the public's craze for all things Washington. He wrote a largely fictional biography that one of his contemporaries described as "eighty pages of as entertaining and edifying matter as can be found in the annals of fanaticism and absurdity." Yet this invented story lives on as an apocryphal lesson about honesty. The reason? It is effective in shaping the behavior of small children.

Parents often lie to kids to encourage them—"Your drawing is wonderful!" or "Your performance in the play was great!" Parents also lie to keep kids from danger. Fairy tales warn children that if they wander off or are disobedient, a witch could grab them. When I was in middle school, teachers warned us kids about the risk of heroin. They convinced me that the merest whiff of street drugs could leave me hopelessly addicted. I remember steering clear of a local park, where rumor had it that addicts sometimes gathered, because I was so terrified about accidentally picking up a deadly addiction. This is a phenomenon that stretches across cultures. One classic study looked at Tzeltal-speaking Mayan corn farmers in southern Mexico. The paper, titled "Everyone Has to Lie in Tzeltal" (a play on Sacks's classic study), recorded a veritable encyclopedia of lies parents told their children to keep them in line. Many involved punishments or consequences that would never actually materialize:

> *The dog/bug/wasp will bite you.*
> *Don't go out on the trail, there are rabid dogs!*
> *I'll take you to the clinic for an injection!*

In the United States, the contradiction between our professed devotion to honesty and our actual dishonesty becomes acute during the holiday season, when a phenomenon surfaces that psychologists call the "undesirable gift paradigm." You have to say you like the gifts you received, especially those from close relatives who put a lot of time and effort (and money) into getting you something unusable or tasteless. It isn't quite right to say we are teaching our kids to be hypocrites. We are teaching them a deeper truth: sometimes, we have to lie in order to be kind.

We also do this with the sick and the elderly. Few people would judge you harshly if you told an elderly parent who wants to drive—but really shouldn't be driving—that her car has broken down and needs fixing, even if the car is just fine. After all, your goal is just to keep your mom from getting in a crash. Some nursing homes take this to an extreme when it comes to patients suffering from dementia, obligingly playing along with fantasies that they are living in the world of their youth. There are even assisted-care facilities designed to look like the towns in which patients grew up. One in Germany mimics East Germany during the Communist era. If these invoke deceptions to soothe agitated patients, surely they are improvements over chair-straps, straitjackets and drugs?

When it comes to adults of sound mind, lying becomes harder to justify. Yet, we often do it, especially to people who are feeling vulnerable in some way. Sometimes we lie to help our associates confront challenges. The old football expression "any given Sunday"—meaning any team can win any game at any time—is often employed by coaches to give even terrible teams the illusion that victory is within grasp. Such illusions can lead to better performance. Studies have shown that people who perceive their goals as attainable perform better than those who think their goals are beyond reach.

Coaches, in fact, tell so many lies to help athletes perform at their best that these lies have become clichés in the sports world. "No one automatically gets a berth. Every position is open to competition" really means, "We want everyone to give us their best shot during training camp, so we can evaluate who the best players are.

But the quarterback and tight end and tackle to whom we have promised to pay fifty million dollars this year are going to play no matter what!" When coaches say, "We're only looking one week ahead," what they really mean is: "All I want you to focus on is next week's game. That's most likely to help us win and, as I think about the whole season, I'm worried I am going to get fired if we don't start winning!" Or consider this favorite saw: "We've got all the pieces, we just have to execute." This can be cover for "We're a terrible team, but that's obvious, so what's the point of beating a dead horse?" In workplaces around the world, managers lie to employees all the time, and the most beloved leaders are often the ones who are most skilled at telling lies. Sometimes these are lies of omission—not telling someone their coworker just received a bonus; sometimes lies of commission—where the difficulty of an impending project is minimized in order to preserve morale.

Of course, we all know deceitful coaches and managers who bring their teams and organizations to ruin, who invite lawsuits for unethical behavior and bullying. When we think about lying, most of us think only of such liars. The other kind, the liars who work to protect the feelings of others, to help them achieve their best and to get back up after they've been knocked down—most of us think highly of those "player's coaches." But if we were to be precise with our language, we might say that the lies we abhor are those where someone says or does something to get ahead at the expense of others, but the lies we admire are those told to help people grow into their best selves, to achieve their fullest potential. Our problem isn't really with deceit—just with who is doing it, why they are doing it, and when.

Most of us tell friends with terminal illnesses or friends going through a divorce that "everything is going to be OK" despite the fact that we don't know that everything will be OK, and sometimes even when we are certain that everything will *not* be OK. We tell our partners they look gorgeous when they don't. We tell colleagues their major setback at work is minor. When my father was dying from cancer some years ago, the physical changes in his body were striking. Each time I saw him, he seemed to be shrinking further in on himself. Yet I tried to maintain a cheerful exterior when I greeted him, and I tried to reassure him that things were going as well as could be expected. I didn't feel such assurance in my own heart. But I felt morally compelled to lie. I knew it made him feel better.

In nearly all of these cases, the same underlying mechanism is at work: It's easy to tell the truth when things are going great, and it's easy to be "brutally honest" to people you dislike. But when people we love experience setbacks, terror or failure, we readily reach for the comforts of deception and self-deception. I would wager that our willingness to practice deception and encourage self-deception rises with the depth of our loyalties, and the extent to which those we care about are experiencing vulnerability. Show me people who have no need for lies, and I will usually show you happy, well-adjusted people whose lives are marked by good health, professional success and material comfort.

All these ideas came to mind recently as I was reporting a story for the *Hidden Brain* podcast and radio show about the opioid crisis in the United States. The story took me to Maryland, where I met a couple named Pete and Hope Troxell. They had been through a terrible tragedy: the death of their adult daughter, Alicia, who was seven months pregnant. Alicia had developed an addiction after being prescribed opioids to treat back pain caused by scoliosis. The medications also eased Alicia's psychological trauma as she went through a difficult divorce. Eventually, she went from taking pre-scription pain medications to heroin. As the drug took over her life, she lost custody of her children, and her pain and suffering at this calamity made her even more dependent on street drugs. When she got pregnant again, Hope and Pete had a "come to Jesus" talk with her. They told her she needed to get her life together for her new baby. They got her into rehab. When she emerged, she moved in with Hope and Pete. One night, after a nice family dinner, Alicia's mother helped her plan clothes for the new baby, whom they were going to name Camden. But the next morning, when Hope came to check on Alicia, she found her propped up in bed, stiff and unresponsive. She had overdosed on a form of synthetic heroin called fentanyl. Hope and Pete tried to resuscitate her, but it was no use. Alicia was dead. Camden was dead, too.

The deaths crushed Hope and Pete. It was a heartbreaking interview, and I found myself in tears as I listened to their story. Then Pete brightened. He told me that as the family was burying Alicia, he looked up and saw an eagle soaring overhead. He remembered a verse from the book of Exodus: "You yourselves have seen what I did to Egypt, and how I carried you on eagles' wings and brought you to myself." Pete felt assured that the eagle was carrying his daughter to heaven.

"When I read that in the Bible I think it made me feel so much better," Pete said, looking at me earnestly. "Even though I lost my daughter, which I hated. In a million years, I didn't think I'd ever lose my kid. They're supposed to bury us. We're not supposed to bury them. But knowing that bald eagle was flying around up there and what the Bible says, it made me feel better knowing that she's in Heaven. Knowing that comfort of hopefully one day I am going to see her and Camden. Every night I go to bed, we go to bed, we say a prayer for him, for her. [We say] Lord, they're in your hands now, you take good care of them. One day we'll see them. It's not 'goodbye,' but 'we'll see you later.' And I think that's what helps get us through this."

Immanuel Kant might have recommended I tell the Troxells that I didn't believe the eagle had anything to do with Alicia, and that the idea that a bird could take a dead person to heaven was ridiculous. The truth was that I believed that this young woman's death was senseless and pointless. It was driven by structural factors far larger than anything we could comprehend in rural Maryland—forces having to do with the destruction wrought by emotional disorders, unethical pharmaceutical industry practices, and the inadequacies of drug treatment in the United States. There was no redemption in the story, no point to the tragedy. The universe does uncaring things all the time. The Troxells were just unlucky.

I said none of those things. Without the slightest hesitation, I nodded at Pete with understanding. I suggested that I agreed with his interpretation, that he was entitled to the peace the story had brought him. You might say it was a lie of omission, not commission. But it was certainly a lie. And looking back, I don't have the slightest regret about it.

Duke professor Dan Ariely is one of the world's foremost experts on the psychology of deception. He's written several books on the ubiquity of lying, and the complicated mechanics that go into our lies. While it has become fashionable in economics to explain deception through a simple cost-benefit analysis—we lie as much as we can to obtain maximum advantage with minimum risk—Ariely has shown that the frequency and scale of our deceptions is usually governed by a search for a moral equilibrium: We want to gain as much advantage as we can while still feeling we are good people. He calls this the "fudge factor."

Most of Ariely's work has revolved around the costs of deception, and how liars and lying can be curtailed. But he has also wrestled with the idea of the *benevolent* lie, where one party wants to be deceived, and a second party, who has the interests of the first in mind, obliges. It turns out that such deceptions and self-deceptions helped Ariely himself during one of the most difficult periods of his life. It might be why he is alive today.

When he was seventeen, Ariely was in a terrible accident. A fireworks display went awry and a flare exploded next to him. Ariely was rushed to the hospital, where he was forced to spend the next three years. "I was in the twelfth grade and plucked out of life," he recalls. The tragedy left him with severe burns over seventy percent of his body. He still routinely requires surgery to treat various complications that stem from the accident.

Ariely calls that period in the hospital his "magnifying glass of life." Like all serious burn victims, he was at a high risk of dying during the first months of the accident. Nobody ever told him this. Nor did they say just how much suffering he would face throughout the rest of his life. "Like everybody that gets injured in a deep way, I also contemplated terminating my life," he told me. "I think if I had at the time a more objective view of what the future would hold, I might have tried to do that. I don't think I could have taken the physicians telling me the truth."

This wasn't the only time the deception of hospital staff helped him. He once had more than a dozen metal nails inserted into his hand as part of a surgical procedure. About three weeks before the nails were due to be removed, he found out that he would be awake and only under local anesthesia during this procedure. The thought terrified him, but a nurse told him that the whole thing would be simple, quick and painless. Three weeks later, Ariely underwent the procedure. It was excruciating. "It turns out it really hurts," he says, able to laugh about it now. "It was painful and took a while to take out these fifteen nails." But the anger Ariely initially felt about being misled by the nurse melted away as he contemplated the alternative. If the nurse had told him the truth, he would have undergone the excruciating surgical procedure *and* suffered weeks of apprehension.

"Think about the three weeks of agony I would have had—of agony, of being afraid," he said. "This way I had the same pain but without the dread that would have come out of it. Now does that justify lying? It's very tough, but I recognize that it contributed to my well-being. When you are a patient, your lack of control and fear is just incredible. You are just lying in bed, other people decide what to do with you, when to do it. And having the fear of people pulling these nails out of me without anesthesia probably would have been very, very difficult to take at the time. I am grateful."

One time, Ariely *was* given the truth—and it was devastating. It happened when the staff arranged what they hoped would be an inspirational visit from a burn victim who was a few years farther down the road to recovery than Ariely. "I had no view of what my future would look like," Ariely told me. "When they brought this patient, he was supposed to symbolize recovery. He was fifteen years after his injury. He looked terrible, with very severe burns. It was clear he didn't have function in his hands—everything I have now. But it was a shock. My own outlook was much more optimistic than that. They brought that patient to show me how life could turn out well. For me it was just a shock to the system."

These experiences left Ariely with the realization that there are circumstances where we must temper our desire to tell the truth with the imperative to protect and comfort. "A couple of years ago, I was asked to help a young guy who was burned," he said. "A relative of his asked me to send this kid an optimistic note about his future. It was tremendous torture for me. On the one hand, I didn't think his future was going to be very optimistic. On the other hand, I didn't think it would be right to expose him to the full brutality of the years ahead of him. I debated for two days while crying quite a lot. Eventually, I found some kind of compromise that I was OK with. It was certainly not the brutal truth straight up."

If you think of benevolent deception and optimistic self-deception not as vice and weakness, but as *adaptive responses* to difficult circumstances, it is not hard to imagine that many of us—confronted by immense pain—might choose the hope of lies over the despair of truth. Of course, that isn't the case with all of us. Some may say, with Immanuel Kant, that truth matters more than hope, health and well-being. But the decks are stacked against these brave souls. Natural selection isn't really interested in the truth. It is interested in *what works*. And your odds of survival are better when you see the world through rose-tinted glasses. At the Mayo Clinic in Rochester, Minnesota, researchers once administered personality tests to five hundred and thirty-four adults suffering from the disease that ultimately killed my father, lung cancer. They divided the patients into two groups, those with an optimistic outlook and those with a pessimistic outlook. They found that the optimists outlived the pessimists by six months.

Now you may say, OK, the optimists do better than the pessimists, but do they fare better than *realists*? Surely, you can be realistic without being pessimistic? A few years before the Mayo Clinic study, another study looked at the life expectancy of seventy-four gay men diagnosed with AIDS. When the study was published in 1994, an AIDS diagnosis was effectively a death sentence. The study found that patients who had a more realistic sense of their disease and its outcomes died *nine months earlier* than patients who had an optimistic view. The researchers titled their paper, "Realistic Acceptance as a Predictor of Decreased Survival Time in Gay Men with AIDS."

In another Mayo Clinic study, researchers provided psychological tests to eight hundred and thirty-nine patients who had come in for all kinds of different medical problems. They tracked these patients over the next thirty years, measuring which patients died and when. They found that a "pessimistic explanatory style" was associated with *a nineteen percent increase* in mortality compared to patients with an "optimistic explanatory style."

If I told you that researchers had discovered a special intervention—absent which human mortality would increase by nineteen percent—but this intervention was being systematically ignored at clinics and hospitals around the world, you would call it medical malpractice. Why is the goal of deliberately boosting hope and optimism not designed into every hospital and medical center? It is because we have bound ourselves in a knot of our own making: Lying is always supposed to be wrong. What if we give people hope and later get accused of encouraging false optimism? By failing to acknowledge that deception and self-deception can sometimes be forces for good, we find ourselves stupefied—and paralyzed—when the evidence points in that direction.

As children of the Enlightenment, we have tethered ourselves to the mast of rationality, to the brilliance of reason. We reject the intuitions, instincts and illogical drives of the ancient faculties of the brain. The truth, we declare, is our only flag; logic is the wind in our sails. And if the wind should blow in the other direction? Our worldview demands that we ignore such evidence.

3

‖‖

The Theater of Healing

It's not a lie if you believe it.

George Costanza, *Seinfeld*

In 1784, a group of some of the world's greatest scientific minds gathered in Paris to investigate a medical device that was hailed around the world as one of the greatest scientific advances in the history of humankind, capable of miraculous healing, even of restoring sight to the blind. This device was essentially a tub of water.

The device, called a *baquet*, was certainly impressive to look at. Constructed out of polished oak, with a nautical-looking hatch, it resembled something out of Jules Verne's *Twenty Thousand Leagues under the Sea*. From its sides protruded eight ornately woven ropes, each paired with a metal rod that rose from the lid and sloped over the sides. By the time the throngs of patients and observers arrived, these rods were magnetized. The invalids would crowd around. Fastened to the device by the ropes, they would press the afflicted parts of their bodies against the magnetic rods. A musician would often join in, playing a glass armonica, an otherworldly-looking instrument made out of spinning goblets that produced haunting, fairy-tinged melodies.

Eventually, the patients would enter a state that believers in the *baquet* reverently called the "crisis." Some patients, the investigators later observed, would "cough, spit, feel slight pain, a warmth either localized or all over, and perspire; others are agitated and tormented by convulsions . . . extraordinary in their number, duration, and strength . . . some lasting for more than three hours" and "accompanied by murky and viscous expectorations. These convulsions are characterized by quick, involuntary movements . . . blurred and unfocused vision, by piercing shrieks, tears, hiccups and excessive laughter. They are preceded or followed by a state of languor and dreaminess." The hysteria would typically escalate with the appearance of the *baquet's* inventor, Franz Anton Mesmer. Tall, handsome and charismatic, he would pace the room in a colorful silk robe and gold slippers, waving a metal wand at patients, or laying his hands on them—usually enough to send them into fresh convulsions.

Mesmer was Austrian by birth, and a graduate of the prestigious University of Vienna. His doctoral dissertation, "The Influence of Planets," was devoted to the effect of planetary bodies on human physiology. He had become interested in magnetism after hearing of miraculous healings performed by an astrologer at the Austrian Royal Court—a priest with the unfortunate name of Maximilian Hell. Soon, Mesmer claimed to have discovered an invisible bodily force he called animal magnetism, which he described as a "mutual influence between the celestial bodies, the earth and the bodies of animated beings." When out of equilibrium, animal magnetism was the source of many physical and mental afflictions. Mesmer claimed his magnetic treatments could cure "epilepsy, melancholia, maniacal attack, and ague," the last term being a catchall for any type of fever.

Paris at the time was under the spell of an array of marvelous scientific discoveries—electricity, gravity, a new understanding of gases that led to flying balloons. Mesmer became the talk of the town. He established two dozen magnetic clinics—called Societies of Harmony—throughout the city. The queen, Marie Antoinette, became a patron, as did the Marquis de Lafayette, hero of the American Revolution, who wrote his friend George Washington to tell him about Mesmer's "great philosophical discovery."

But the late eighteenth century was also a time of increasing scientific scrutiny. Not everyone was convinced by Mesmer's miraculous new healing art. Many scientists were skeptical of animal magnetism. Mesmer himself petitioned for an official inquiry to prove or disprove his claims of magnetic healing. He wrote to the Society of Medicine and threw down a challenge: He asked them to select two dozen patients. He would treat half of them, and regular physicians would treat the remainder. The experiment would reveal who was more successful. The Society basically ignored him. But not long after, an intruder claiming to be "bewitched" by Mesmer broke into Louis XVI's bedroom, and the king decided to take action. He appointed a commission made up of some of France's greatest scientists, including, most prominently, the man still remembered as the father of modern chemistry, Antoine Lavoiser, who coined the terms oxygen and hydrogen. To lead the commission, the king tapped Benjamin Franklin, the enormously popular American ambassador in Paris, whose investigations into the nature of electricity had become legendary in France. (Franklin was also, coincidentally, the inventor of the glass armonica used in Mesmer's *baquet* sessions.)

This time, Mesmer declined to take part in the investigation. The commissioners never actually met with him, and made do instead with one of Mesmer's chief disciples, Charles d'Eslon, physician to the king's brother, through whom the commissioners were able to examine all of the magnetic healing methods practiced by Mesmer, including the *baquet*.

Some investigators allowed themselves to be treated by d'Eslon. None of them felt anything, certainly not the extreme sensations experienced by patients bound to the *baquet*. The investigators then devised a series of clever experiments to test whether the patients were truly responding to animal magnetism—or to something else. In one, a patient was seated in front of a closed door behind which, she was told, d'Eslon was magnetizing her. He was not in fact present. "After three minutes," the commissioners wrote, the woman "stretched both arms behind her back, twisting them strongly, and bending her body forward. Her whole body shook. The chatter of teeth was so loud that it could be heard from outside; she bit her hand hard enough to leave teeth marks." Another patient was blindfolded and led through Franklin's garden where d'Eslon had "magnetized" a tree. As the patient was led further from the actual tree, he appeared to experience the effects of magnetism more acutely until, the commissioners observed, "he lost consciousness, his limbs stiffened and he was carried to a nearby lawn where M. d'Eslon gave him first aid."

The report concluded that no force such as animal magnetism existed. In the eyes of many, Mesmer was exposed as a fraud who preyed on the weak-minded. His reputation shattered, he eventually left the country. Today, the experiments that debunked Franz Mesmer are usually remembered as the first placebo-controlled studies of a medical treatment. The investigators had devised a series of clever traps to expose a charlatan. Science had won out over superstition. The conclusion of many who followed the proceedings was that Mesmer's wands and the *baquet* didn't work.

That was not entirely true. A few years before Benjamin Franklin was tasked with leading the investigation of Mesmer, a sick man had written to him for advice on whether he should visit one of Mesmer's magnetic clinics. Such cures, Franklin wrote, were based on "delusion" and "a disposition in mankind to deceive themselves." Yet Franklin said it still might be worth the trip because "delusion may, however, in some cases, be of use . . . there are in every great city a number of persons who are never in health, because they are fond of medications, and by always taking them, hurt their constitutions. If these people can be persuaded to forbear their drugs in expectation of being cured by only the physician's finger or an iron rod pointing at them, they may possibly find good effects."

This was essentially what Franklin and his fellow commissioners eventually said about Mesmer. They had been charged with determining whether animal magnetism actually existed as a force akin to, say, electricity. But even as they concluded it was not, many accepted that Mesmer's patients were in fact healed. The source of the healing lay not in animal magnetism, or in Mesmer's wands or tubs, but in the drama of the cures and in the imaginations of the patients themselves. "The action and the reaction of the physical upon the mental and of the mental upon the physical, have been demonstrated since observation has been part of Medicine," they wrote in their final report. The commissioners described this process as the power of "imagination."

Mesmer himself seems to have come to see his magnetic healings in much the same way. In his later years, he increasingly saw the physical elements of his healing techniques as unnecessary, instead attributing his healing capabilities simply to the force of his own personality (which is, ironically, what we mean today when we use the term "animal magnetism"). The cure lay in the *theater* of magnetic healing, an elaborate deception designed to play on the patient's expectations, to harness the patient's own capacity to heal. At a time when leeching, cutting and burning were common medical practices, and when school children were encouraged to smoke tobacco for its supposed health benefits, treatment by Mesmer's tubs and wands was relatively benign (his Societies of Harmony strictly banned the use of tobacco). Had the Paris medical establishment accepted Mesmer's initial challenge, there is a good chance he might have won. At the very least, his treatments might have caused patients less harm than the standard medical treatments of the day.

In 1994, more than two centuries after the debunking of Anton Mesmer, an American surgeon named Bruce Moseley prepared to perform an arthroscopic knee surgery in the operating theater of the Houston Veterans Affairs Medical Center. The term "operating theater" often seems like an anachronism, a remnant of the early days of surgery, when operations were performed before large crowds in actual theaters—often accompanied, like Mesmer's *baquet* treatments, by musicians. But in the case of the procedure Moseley was about to perform, the term was particularly apt.

After Moseley scrubbed in, the anesthetized patient—a middle-aged man with arthritic knees—was wheeled in. Moseley was handed an envelope with a note inside informing him that the man was part of a placebo group. Moseley began the procedure as he normally would, by making three pen-sized incisions in the patient's knee. He then turned his attention to a television set that had been placed prominently next to the operating table. On it, Moseley could see a video of himself performing a real arthroscopy. He proceeded to mimic his actions on screen. "If I was looking in one compartment of the knee, I would have the leg positioned that way," he later recalled to me. "If I put something in the knee on the videotape, I would actually ask for that instrument and pretend like I was doing something. So I moved the leg around, I would pass the leg around, I would move instruments like we were doing the real thing." However, Moseley never performed any of the tasks that would constitute the actual surgery. Aside from the initial incision, he never inserted any of his surgical instruments into the patient.

The procedure was part of a study Moseley developed shortly after his arrival in Houston. When he was serving his residency in Salt Lake City, he had been taught that arthroscopies for arthritis were useless. But in Houston, he found the operation was performed for that condition all the time. Some surgeons speculated that the reason the procedure was effective wasn't from the mechanical scraping of residue from the knee—the actual goal of the operation—but because surgeons flushed the knee joint with saline solution—which allowed them to see what they were doing during the procedure. Moseley wanted to test this idea by giving one group the actual operation, while only flushing the knees of patients in a second group. A colleague suggested he add a third arm to the study, a placebo group.

Moseley was flabbergasted. He had been surgeon for the Houston Rockets, where he treated NBA stars like Hakeem Olajuwon and Charles Barkley. Placebo surgery was not something he had ever considered. For him as for most doctors—and most people— the image conjured by the word "placebo" was that of a sugar pill. It didn't have anything to do with surgery or, for that matter, *real* medicine. But then he started to educate himself on the subject. The more he read, the more he understood that the placebo effect could play a role in surgery. The effect could be greatest when patients felt the perceived intervention was largest. "If it's a small pill, sometimes the effect is not as great as a bigger pill," he explained. "Or if it's a 'new and exciting' pill, there's probably more of a placebo effect than an old and traditional pill." Surgery, with its reputation as a treatment of last resort, might exert far more influence on a patient than even the largest pill.

At first, hospital administrators bristled at the idea of one of their doctors performing sham surgery. But eventually Moseley got the go-ahead. Although offering fake surgery might have seemed like a hard sell to patients, Moseley found willing participants—arthritis patients who had run out of options when it came to their aching knees. "We actually had them sign a piece of paper that said 'I understand that I might get randomized to a placebo group, and placebo means pretend, and if I'm in this group, that means I might get a pretend surgery,'" says Moseley. "They had to write it in their own handwriting to make sure they understood everything we were saying."

The results were remarkable. Two years after their procedures, patients who received actual surgeries, those who got the saline wash and those who received placebo surgeries all reported a marked level of improvement. And there were no differences in the level of improvement between the patients in any of the groups. Moseley called the results "jaw dropping." A subsequent and larger study confirmed the results. Arthroscopic surgery is one of the most common surgical procedures in the world. In cases where it was being performed to treat arthritis, Moseley's experiment proved that the beneficial effects could be traced entirely to the placebo effect.

The placebo has been part of the physician's toolkit since the earliest days of medicine. Plato noted a physician's power to heal through "words and phrases." In Mesmer's time, placebos were commonplace. Thomas Jefferson once confided that "one of the most successful physicians I have ever known has assured me that he used more of bread pills, drops of colored water, and powders of hickory ashes, than of all other medicines put together."

Yet most physicians did not really understand just how much healing could be achieved through these acts of deception. A nineteenth-century compendium of medical terms defined *placebo*—from the Latin for "to please"—as "medicine adapted more to please than to benefit the patient." It wasn't until the 1960s, when the FDA mandated more stringent testing of new drugs and placebo-controlled studies became *de rigueur*, that we started to quantify just how much modern pharmaceuticals owed to the placebo effect. For instance, substantial numbers of people who suffer from depression get better in clinical trials when they are given antidepressants. But lots of patients in these trials also get better when they receive sugar pills.

You might say, OK, this means the drugs tested were ineffective. But no, we're talking about drugs that have now been prescribed to millions of people, drugs that many people credit with saving their lives. These are drugs touted in pharmaceutical company advertising as very effective. What this suggests is that a significant portion of the benefit of these drugs in the real world also arises from the placebo effect. While it's true that the placebo effect is strongest in chronic conditions that involve pain or mental suffering—depression, say, or arthritis—there are few treatments that do not owe at least some of their success to the placebo effect.

The placebo effect is often described as the effect of mind over matter. But it is actually about something much more powerful: the power of the drama and rituals embedded in the practice of medicine—a theater that involves (often at an unconscious level) deception on the part of the physician and self-deception on the part of the patient. I remember when I was a small child, I would see a kindly family physician. Even at the time, I remember noticing something curious: The moment he appeared, I would start to feel better. As he listened patiently to me, I could feel myself start to relax. Many years later, as I covered mental health issues at the *Washington Post*, I learned that one of the best predictors of positive outcomes in psychotherapy was not the kind of therapy being administered, but the bond of trust that exists between doctor and patient.

A great deal of the suffering caused by disease is caused by our own reactions to illness: Our anxiety and worry about the ailments we have, and what it *means* to be sick. When my family doctor appeared, his presence didn't eliminate the virus that had brought me down, or the bacterial infection that had triggered a fever. But he eased my worry and anxiety. He communicated the powerful message we all want to hear when we are unwell: "Don't worry, I'm here now. I will look after you." These same factors are at play in almost every healing situation. The placebo effect is likely strongest in cases like surgery, where a patient surrenders entirely to a doctor, often consenting to be unconscious during a procedure. There is a great deal of preparation before surgery, a heightening of expectation, a feeling that one is undertaking the most sophisticated of potential treatments. The patient is literally putting his or her life in the doctor's hands. It is no small step to "go under the knife." The operating theater is undoubtedly one of the most dramatic forms of *theater*.

We may laugh at "primitive" cultures where the sick are treated by "witch doctors," without realizing that when we walk into modern hospitals, with their high-tech machines, sophisticated monitors and white-coated physicians, we are in fact enacting our own version of the witch doctor's cures. Obviously, this is not to say all of medicine is just drama and ritual. If you are seriously sick, you want to be treated at the Mayo Clinic, not by a wizard with a wand.

You should prefer an antidepressant that has been approved by the FDA, not a concoction brewed by your aunt. But it is to say that some part of the benefit you get from the antidepressant or from the Mayo Clinic *is* about theater.

Bruce Moseley, the doctor who performed the fake arthritis operation, has taken this lesson to heart. He has come to realize that his job is not done when he emerges from surgery. He now remembers, after he finishes an operation, to communicate to the patient and to the patient's family that everything has gone exceptionally well, that a good outcome is all but assured. He knows his confidence will translate into their confidence. Their optimism—their *hope*—is part of the cure.

For several centuries, going all the way back to Benjamin Franklin and Anton Mesmer, the placebo has been used in medicine primarily to separate what works from what doesn't. This has helped to weed out charlatans, and to better gauge the actual effects of treatments. Unfortunately, when a placebo-controlled study shows that a sugar pill works as well as a drug, most people simply conclude that the drug "doesn't work." That isn't necessarily true. When patients in the placebo arm of a clinical trial do as well as those in the treatment arm of a trial, it would be more accurate to say, "The effect of this drug is limited to the placebo effect."

As we have seen, that effect is far from zero. Many of us, however, are unwilling to even consider the next question: If the placebo effect can help people, why are we not using it widely across all of medicine? That is a question that Ted Kaptchuk, Director of the Program in Placebo Studies and the Therapeutic Encounter at Harvard University, has been asking for a long time. "If fifty percent of people got better by placebo, and fifty percent by a drug, it's a failed trial," he says. "They are missing that fifty percent of people got better."

Consider a 1959 study by Seattle cardiologist Leonard Cobb that showed a popular surgery for angina, internal mammary artery ligation—tying off arteries to increase the blood flow to the heart— was no more effective than a placebo surgery where the arteries were not tied. For decades, the surgery had been considered incredibly effective: Seventy-five percent of patients undergoing the procedure showed improvement, and a third were deemed cured. Yet the response to Cobb's results was to stop doing the surgery, meaning that we now refuse to give patients recourse to something that helped many people.

Of course, providing such surgery would come with thorny ethical, political and financial dilemmas. If we were to start giving patients treatments that are no better than a placebo, only in order to generate the placebo effect, doesn't this open the door to every merchant of snake oil, every modern Anton Mesmer? Would the placebo effect even work if people came to believe their doctors were routinely prescribing placebos—or does eliciting the placebo effect depend on doctors *deceiving* patients into imagining that they are getting "real" medications? Does it depend on doctors *themselves* believing that the cures work?

Kaptchuk has thought long and hard about these questions. He is an expert on the complex interplay of rituals and beliefs that make up the foundation of what we call the placebo effect. A lot of his knowledge stems from his work on placebos at Harvard. But it also comes from his unique background in healing. As a youth, Kaptchuk, a self-styled "product of the '60s," wanted to find a career where nobody could accuse him of "working for the man." He ended up studying traditional Chinese medicine in Macau, Taiwan and mainland China. "I learned herbs and acupuncture," he says. "I trained in how do you prescribe formulas, how do you diagnose Yin and Yang and find elements and dampness and wind. Eventually, I got good enough that I could tell if a person had wind the way you would look at my shirt and say, 'That's a blue shirt.'"

When Kaptchuk returned to the United States, he set up a practice in Boston, on a street known as "Quack Row." His neighbors included chiropractors, an array of energy healers, a past-life regressionist and a Jamaican healer who administered cures in the form of brightly colored waters. Kaptchuk's office fit right in. "I had at least two or three hundred herbs in jars all over the waiting room," he says. "I had wonderful pictures of China. Some of the herbs were parts of lizards and geckos and seahorses, the kinds of things that were very exotic and probably had symbolic value."

Kaptchuk was successful—so successful, in fact, that patients would tell him that he had cured them of conditions he wasn't even aware that they had. He began to question what was really happening. "I'd say, 'That's interesting. I didn't give them any herbs for that,'" he says. "And I realized that something else is going on here. I started looking at some of these Chinese medical texts, and they would say the medicine should start working before the patient takes the herbs. Chinese medicine doesn't talk about doctor-patient relations at all. But I realized that there was something else going on other than herbs and acupuncture. And I wasn't sure how to interpret that yet."

Eventually Kaptchuk realized that it was his interactions with patients, the elaborate theater of healing, that was paving the way for people to get better. "I'd see people walk into my office, sit down with me," he says. "We talk for fifteen minutes. Half hour. We have a meaningful conversation. I ask about their life, their illness. I felt their pulse. As they walked out, I saw them walking with less pain, more bounce in their gait. And I told myself, 'Ted, you just changed that person.' That was not the herbs. The herbs may or may not have helped more. But I saw there was something going on that I hadn't been taught about in any depth in China. It was a constellation of the rituals and behaviors of medicine. It involves words, silence, attentive listening, building trust. It mostly involves hope. I think I saw something that we will call in biomedicine the placebo effect."

Later, after Kaptchuk was recruited by Harvard, he went on to study statistics and epidemiology, and was, in his words, "rehabilitated." But in regular Western medicine—what he means by "biomedicine"—he saw the same forces at play when a patient visits a doctor. Kaptchuk has conducted studies showing that placebos can be deliberately used to cure patients. Some of his more groundbreaking work explores the idea that the placebo effect can be harnessed even when a patient is *explicitly told* that they are being given placebos. Again, this underlines something easily overlooked—when you get a prescription for pills, it isn't just the pills that do the curing. It's everything else, too—your visit to the doctor, the effort it took to make an appointment, the drama of the doctor's waiting room, the ability of the doctor to listen attentively to you, the medical center's efforts to put you at ease. Even when you are told you are getting a placebo, meaning there is no chemical substance that is acting upon your body, all of the other elements of drama are still intact—and ought to still work.

Kaptchuk bristles at the idea that such theater is a form of deception. "Honesty is core to the moral code of medicine," he says. Now, doctors might not be explicitly lying and patients might not be explicitly deceived during everyday medical interventions, but I would argue there are certainly *implicit* acts of deception and self-deception at hospitals and doctors' offices that contribute to the success of treatment. What takes place in these settings is hardly different than what happens at an actual theater. When you go to see a play, you understand your experience is going to be heightened if you suspend a certain amount of disbelief. When you watch a movie and it says that ten years have passed between scenes, you go along with this fiction because you understand that this belief makes the story work—*and you want the story to work*. It's exactly the same in medicine. There are unspoken complicities of deception and self-deception that allow the drama and rituals of medicine to have their full effect. In the case of serious medical conditions where the placebo effect can do good—and even save lives—it is not a stretch to call the placebo the most benevolent of lies. The medical ethicist Howard Brody has called the placebo "the lie that heals."

At least one survey has shown that the general public is open to the idea of more widespread use of placebos. The problem is that sanctioning their use requires us to come up with a nuanced way to talk about deception and self-deception. It's exactly like the coaches and managers we discussed earlier. Few companies would ever set up policies that explicitly permit deception, because that would open them up to criticism and lawsuits. But prohibiting all deception and self-deception—were such policies to ever be actually put into practice—can throw the baby out with the bathwater. It would certainly be difficult to preserve only those deceptions and self-deceptions that produce useful outcomes, while eliminating the ones that are harmful. It would be next to impossible to write medical guidelines that tell doctors they can lie under some circumstances. But because we don't want to engage with the complexity of these questions, and because we want to pretend that effective policies can be painted in black and white terms—lying is bad, telling the truth is good—we are left with this irony: Many doctors realize that the efficacy of their treatments depends on the theater of medicine. But they are allowed to capitalize on this only if such deception is practiced "under the table," without anyone acknowledging that it is happening.

. . .

Long before modern medicine was invented, long before humans arrived on the planet, animals suffered injuries and fell sick. Swordfish and tortoises didn't have CT scans and X-ray machines. So the brains of animals did what brains everywhere are designed to do—they used what they had around them to make do. For many species, especially social species like elephants, wolves and chimpanzees, algorithms in the brain learned, through trial and error over millions of years, to prompt creatures to turn to the loving care of others when confronted by illness or injury. Doing this did not constitute a cure, at least in the way we define cures. But it probably increased the odds of survival. A baby elephant that turned to her mother in distress was more likely to survive than a baby elephant that chose to go off by herself, or was ignored by her kin. Over time, aspects of the brain that caused animals to turn to others for help, to trust others in times of need—and that prompted caregivers to deliver comfort and protection to loved ones—were *conserved*.

This is why every person knows today, when they or their children are sick, that illness and injury can draw families and communities together. The ancient algorithms in the brain that tell us to turn to others for help, that draw others to our aid, these do not go away simply because we now have high-tech hospitals and powerful drugs. This is why, all over the world, people crave from their doctors what we always crave in the face of suffering: understanding, patience and compassion. When we construct modern medical systems using only logic and rationality—and all of us have been to such facilities—we certainly benefit from the discoveries of science and medicine, but we instinctively know we are a long way from the balm of healing.

4

IIIIIIIIIIIIIIIIIIIIIIIIIIIIIIIIIIIIIIIIIIIIIIIIIIIIIIIIIIIIIIIIIIIIIIIIIIIIIIIIIIIIIIIIIIIIIIIIIIIIIIIIIIIIIIIIIIIIIIIIIIIIIIIIIII

The Invisible Hand

There is nothing either good or bad, but thinking makes it so.

William Shakespeare, *Hamlet*

A 2003 episode of *Bullshit*—a television show in which the magicians Penn and Teller set about exposing and dissecting various forms of fraud and delusion—was set in a posh California restaurant. It had its own "water steward," who was like a sommelier, except with fancy bottled water standing in for wine. Diners were presented with a leather-bound water menu, with detailed descriptions to suit the most discriminating connoisseur. *L'eau du Robinet* (French for "tap water") was described as "pure, brisk and unmistakably French" with an "aggressive flavor and brash attitude that make it a perfect complement to meats and poultry." A bottle of *Amazon*—produced "by the Brazilian rain forest's natural filtration system"—contained an "Amazonian arachnid," like the worm at the bottom of a bottle of mezcal. *Mt. Fuji* was "known throughout the Far East for its clean and bracing flavor as well as its restorative powers as a natural diuretic and anti-toxin." It tasted, one diner gushed, of "a glacier." The same diner was even more effusive about the *Agua de Culo* (Spanish for "ass water"), which was served at the end of the meal. He noted it had a particularly pronounced "kick."

As you might have guessed by the name of the show, the water steward was an actor. The water in the fancy bottles was drawn from a garden hose. It was a charade designed to highlight the stupidity of paying for water that was, were it not for the bottle and the setting and the price, indistinguishable from the water used to spray down the patio.

But were the excellent reviews just baloney? If people went home thinking they had just drunk the most magnificent cup of water—perhaps recalling "this amazing water" at future dinner parties—did it really matter if it came from a garden hose? If I think something is amazing and am willing to pay top dollar for it, does it really matter that you think it's "bullshit"? Penn and Teller suggested that the reactions of the diners were simply a case of the Emperor's New Clothes: They raved about the water because that was what was expected of them. They reacted the way they were *supposed* to react when being served an expensive water drawn from Mount Fuji. They acted impressed because they didn't want to look unrefined. But notice the leap in logic. It is certainly the case that the water wasn't special. However, when we assume that the diners thought it was special only because they didn't want to look stupid, we are assuming the taste of water is only about its physical properties. If drama and theater and expectations can change the outcome of patients suffering from arthritis, can't it do the same for diners in a restaurant?

The psychological factors behind the placebo effect in medicine are, in fact, *around us all the time*. They shape nearly every decision we make as consumers, whether it is clicking to buy something on Amazon, or seizing upon a great deal at a thrift shop. In fact, modern economies rely heavily on a secret ingredient: Storytelling. When you buy a diamond ring, or you sell shares in a company, or you accept money in exchange for a service, *you are trading in stories*.

Most of the time, these stories are invisible to us; we go about our lives as economic actors imagining the things we buy and sell are not stories, but concrete reality. But there are times when the artifice behind our transactions—behind money itself—is brought sharply into view. A few years ago, in a bid to go after unaccounted wealth, the government of India declared that more than eighty percent of all the currency in circulation the previous day was worthless. The old currency notes were now just colored paper. The idea was that people who were hiding wads of cash in their bedrooms would have to come out of the shadows, or forfeit their wealth. Overnight, money was revealed for what it really is— a shared story whose value rests entirely on collective beliefs and mutual trust. (For a brief window, the government allowed people to trade their now-worthless currency notes for new legal tender— i.e., a new story.) Similar things happen in the aftermath of war, when currency notes from an old regime go from being a valuable possession to worthless paper. After the countries of Europe decided to abandon their various separate currencies for a common euro, I failed to exchange some old deutsche marks. Now, I'm left with paper that used to mean something, but doesn't anymore. The paper hasn't changed, but *the story* embedded in my deutsche marks has changed, transforming the notes from something valuable into a mere curiosity.

In exactly the same fashion, two glasses of water may have the same chemical makeup. But when we imbue one glass of water with expectation and suggestion—that is, when we give it a good story— it changes, becoming something altogether new. This is why people who eat meat labeled seventy-five percent fat-free will report that it tastes better than meat labeled twenty-five percent fat. There is a reason companies around the world spend more than half a trillion dollars every year on advertising.

When asked why we like the things we like, most of us quickly come up with plausible and reasonable answers. We say we enjoy our iPhones because of their design, efficiency and ease of use. But some of our enjoyment also has to do with the fact that Apple spends about two *billion* dollars a year to persuade people that its products are cool and special. Once Apple manages to convince us that our iPhones are not just phones but devices with uncanny magic, the phones make us happier than if we thought of them as mere phones. The objects that populate our lives are more than the sum of their physical parts.

In the case of pharmaceuticals, people respond better to a new and exciting drug than they do to one that is old and familiar, even if the two drugs are basically identical. Both doctors and patients dance to the tune of seductive medical "breakthroughs." Physicians want to prescribe medications derived from "cutting-edge" research. Patients want treatments that are new and exciting. Pharmaceutical company advertising—often featuring stories of lovers walking through meadows or animals frolicking with their elderly but active owners—not only increases sales, but has been found to increase the efficacy of the drugs by heightening the placebo effect. You aren't just buying pills; the Viagra ads you watch on TV help you believe you can buy vitality, youth and vigor.

Transactions in the marketplace really operate on two different levels. There is the ordinary level—you buy a pill, and you keep taking it if it works. If you feel better, you say it is because of the chemical properties of the pill. Simultaneously, however, there is another transaction taking place, one that usually flies under the radar, but is in many ways just as powerful. It involves a series of deceptions and self-deceptions between you and a multibillion-dollar drug company. Neither of you explicitly acknowledges this second transaction. Pfizer doesn't say, "Our drug is designed to trick you into believing you have stopped the march of time." And you don't say, "Viagra allows me to deceive myself into thinking I am twenty-five again." In fact, the seduction works best when neither side acknowledges it is happening, and when both sides believe their deceptions and self-deceptions are not deceits at all.

There are lots of techniques that companies use to construct the stories behind their products. Perhaps the simplest is the one employed by Penn and Teller in *Bullshit*: If you want to heighten people's expectations of a product, just raise its price.

In 1984, a shuttered General Motors auto plant in Fremont, California, reopened as part of a joint venture between the American car company and Toyota. The Japanese company was looking for a manufacturing toehold in the United States and wanted to learn more about the U.S. market, while GM wanted to study Japanese manufacturing techniques. Instead of building a brand-new car, the plant simply rebranded one of Toyota's existing models, the Corolla, which GM then sold as the Geo Prizm.

The Toyota Corolla and the Geo Prizm were based on the same design, built from similar materials, and put together by the same workers at the very same plant. For all intents and purposes, they were the same car. They performed identically in the eyes of professional critics. It stood to reason that they should have been equally popular with consumers. But as the years unfolded, three things differentiated the Toyota Corolla from the Geo Prizm. First, the Corolla vastly outsold the Prizm. Second, and more surprising, drivers of the Corolla reported fewer maintenance problems than Prizm drivers. Finally, Corolla drivers reported being happier with their cars than Prizm owners.

There was one important difference between the Geo Prizm and the Toyota Corolla: the *price*. The Corolla cost about two thousand dollars more than the Prizm. (Oddly, Prizms weren't just cheaper to begin with. They also went on to depreciate faster than Corollas: After five years, the average Prizm lost five hundred and twenty dollars more in value than the average Corolla, according to an analysis by Duke University marketing professor Debu Purohit.) You might think it unsurprising that customers paid more for a car that said "Toyota" on the nameplate—brand names matter. It doesn't necessarily make rational sense, but again, this shows you how *the story* that products tell is an important part of what consumers are willing to pay for. But why would the cars have different depreciation rates, and why would Prizm owners report more maintenance problems? The cars were metal and paint, cables, screws and wires. They were the stuff of physical reality, not psychological legerdemain. Between 1990 and 1997, drivers who were asked to rate their Corollas and Prizms on engine reliability, transmission, drive and fuel system, and body hardware, gave the Prizm a four-out-of-five rating while the Corolla received a five out of five—a twenty percent difference between cars that were basically identical.

I'll answer those questions in a minute, but let me first lay out some other aspects of the strange relationship between the price of a product and the value we derive from it. The power of price to affect our experience of consumer products reaches far beyond big-ticket purchases like automobiles. Take wine, for instance. I know very little about wine but, like most consumers, I am anxious not to let my dinner guests know that I am an ignoramus. I recently bought a case of wine at a store that allowed me to mix and match a dozen bottles. As I picked bottles, I paid close attention to how I selected them: I chose six reds and six whites. I read the labels, although I didn't really understand them. I asked a store clerk about a couple of my choices, and he was generally enthusiastic about all my selections—I suppose, in dealing with ignorami, it makes little sense to explain why particular choices are stupid. I confess I like bottles with attractively designed labels, and I assumed older wine was superior to bottles of recent vintage. The one thing I tried hard not to do was to link the quality of wine bottles with their price.

If my wine buying expedition was more cautious and deliberate than usual, it was because I had just heard about an interesting experiment conducted by an economist at the California Institute of Technology. Antonio Rangel and his colleagues invited occasional wine drinkers to a tasting. He placed before them wine from multiple bottles that ranged in price from five dollars to ninety dollars. Without the knowledge of the wine drinkers, however, Rangel and his colleagues arranged for the wine in the ten-dollar bottle and the ninety dollar-bottle to be identical—they *both* contained the ten-dollar wine.

This experiment might well have been labeled "Revenge of the Ignoramuses." You can probably guess what happened next. When Rangel asked the volunteers to judge the quality of the wine in the different bottles, people who took a few sips from the ninety-dollar bottle (that really contained ten-dollar wine) smacked their lips and declared it was superior to the wine from the bottle correctly labeled as ten-dollar wine.

As my fellow ignoramuses chortle, I should mention that there is a wide body of similar experiments that have found that people employ the same rule of thumb for any number of products, including food and clothing. This rule of thumb that things that cost more must be superior to things that cost less is an example of what scientists call a "heuristic," a mental shortcut. Heuristics are often useful. If I know nothing about two products except their price, it is reasonable to assume that the more expensive product is the better product. A Toyota Lexus costs much more than a Corolla; it is also widely seen as a better car. The problem with heuristics is that clever marketers can exploit our mental shortcuts and sell us Corollas that are identical to Prizms at a premium of two thousand dollars. Corolla buyers assume the higher priced (and better branded) car is the superior car, just like wine drinkers assume that higher priced wine is superior wine.

But it turns out that it was wine connoisseurs who had the last laugh in the Rangel experiment. The researchers conducted brain imaging scans of the volunteers and found something unexpected: When volunteers tasted the ten-dollar wine from the ninety-dollar bottle, a part of their brains lit up more than when they tasted the same wine from a ten-dollar bottle. This part of the brain, known as the medial orbitofrontal cortex, is activated when people experience pleasure. To put it another way, people seemed to be *experiencing* more pleasure when drinking the ten-dollar wine from the ninety-dollar bottle, than when drinking the ten-dollar wine from the ten-dollar bottle. They were not simply deducing that the expensive wine was better—to them, it actually *tasted better*. The wine in the bottles was identical, but people derived more pleasure from the expensively packaged wine.

"In other words, your expectations actually turn into reality," said study coauthor and Stanford University behavioral economist Baba Shiv. "If I expect the ninety-dollar bottle of wine to taste better, the area of the brain that shows pleasure in real time shows greater activation."

The experiment raises a disturbing question for me (and other wine ignoramuses). We might think that connoisseurs who pay premium prices for wine are suckers, but if these people derive more pleasure because they paid more, are they being cheated—or getting their money's worth? The point of a bottle of wine *is*, after all, to produce subjective pleasure. Does it really matter if this subjective pleasure is produced because the wine in two bottles is objectively different, or because people experience more pleasure when they pay extra for the same wine? To put it another way, regardless of whether your enjoyment comes from the physical properties of the wine or the *story* of the wine, isn't the money you pay producing heightened pleasure?

Other research Baba Shiv has worked on shows that price not only increases our enjoyment of things, it can also tangibly increase the boost we get from products. Some years ago, he and his colleagues recruited fitness fanatics from a local gym. The psychologists gave their volunteers an energy drink known as Twinlab Ultra Fuel. One group of exercisers was told that the psychologists purchased their drink at two dollars and eighty-nine cents, while volunteers in another group were told the regular price of the drink was two dollars and eighty-nine cents but that the psychologists had snagged it at a discount price of eighty-nine cents. The volunteers were then allowed to work out as usual, and later asked to rate the quality of their exercising on a series of scales. Although people said it was impossible that the price of the drink would affect the quality of their workout, the rating scales showed that people who drank the discounted drink had workouts of lower intensity than those who got the drink at full price. Not only that, people who drank the "cheap" version reported on the scales that they felt more fatigued after their workouts than people who drank the "full-priced" version.

In a second experiment, the researchers gave a number of volunteers a drink that supposedly boosts mental performance—SoBe Adrenaline Rush. Volunteers were led to believe the drink would boost their mental sharpness. These volunteers, unlike the previous group, had to pay for their own drinks. But as before, some volunteers got their drink at the full price—in this case, one dollar eighty-nine cents—while others were allowed to buy the drink at the discounted price of eighty-nine cents. The volunteers were then given a booklet with fifteen puzzles and told they had thirty minutes to come up with solutions.

The puzzles were word jumbles. T-U-P-P-I-L, for example, had to be unjumbled to form PULPIT. The letters B-E-R-K-A-M had to be unjumbled to form EMBARK. This time, the researchers did not rely on volunteers' reports about how well they performed, but simply measured something objective: How many puzzles did people in the two groups solve in the allotted time?

In any rational universe, you would expect that there would be no difference in the number of puzzles solved by the group that got SoBe Adrenaline Rush at regular price and the group that got the drink at a discount. Volunteers had been divided at random into two groups. There should have been wordsmiths in both groups who solved the puzzles with ease, and there should have been people in both groups who threw up their hands in frustration. If there was any difference between the groups, it should have been minor—just the random possibility that one group happened to have more word-puzzle enthusiasts.

But the difference in performance between the groups was far from trivial. The people who drank the full-priced drink solved nearly *twice* as many puzzles as those who got the drink on discount. (As you might expect, volunteers in this experiment rejected the possibility that their performance was influenced by the price of the drink.) "It was amazing," Shiv confessed to me in an interview.

The tales of these consumer products—the Toyota Corolla and the Geo Prizm, the cheap and expensive wine, and the full-price and discounted energy drink—all revolve around the "price-placebo effect," a phenomenon where people who pay more for something experience the thing differently than if they pay less.

It doesn't just explain subjective differences, such as how much we enjoy our glass of chardonnay, but objective differences, like how many puzzles we solve when we pay full price for a drink, or how well a more expensive Toyota Corolla is seen to perform compared to a cheaper duplicate.

Why did Corolla owners report fewer maintenance problems with their cars compared to Prizm owners? Duke University marketing professor Debu Purohit thinks that Corolla owners attached greater value to their cars than Geo Prizm owners because they had paid more. When it came time to change the oil, rotate the tires and fix minor problems, Toyota owners were probably more diligent about getting those things done promptly, because they valued their cars more. Prizm owners valued their cars less because they paid less, and this difference eventually produced objectively measurable differences in the condition of used Corollas and Prizms. Psychological differences eventually produced physical differences: Used Prizms depreciated faster than their more expensive twins.

Price is only one signal of quality. There are other ways companies can communicate the story of their products. Brands, as we have seen, can have a particularly powerful effect on the way we experience a product. They can represent in the minds of consumers what Wharton School marketing professor Americus Reed calls a "meaning system." When customers identify closely with a brand, they can come to feel that the brand is an extension of "who they are." Reed likes to use the Apple iPod as an example.

"The iPod is a made-up concept," he told me in an interview. "But Apple was smart enough to tell a story that the iPod was somehow endowed with some sort of self-expressive utility that makes it different from an MP3 player, even though an iPod *is* just another

MP3 player. And so they actually created a psychological distinction by creating a term that was made up and then endowing that
term with all of the Apple self-expressive brand-based thoughts
and ideas about creativity, and hip and cool and fun and sexy design
and all of these things."

Our attachments to brands—to a "Ford-tough" truck, for
example, or the racially harmonious "United Colors" of the clothes
maker Benetton—is testament to the power of storytelling in consumer life. Reed learned this lesson for himself during what he
describes as a "bittersweet moment." After knee problems forced
him to give up playing basketball, he took up cycling to stay active.
Reed says he "fell in love" with Lance Armstrong and his "Live-
Strong" brand. Reed adored Armstrong's story—the cyclist fought
off cancer to win the grueling *Tour de France* seven times. Before
getting on his own bike, Reed would be sure to put on a LiveStrong
bracelet—"I had about fifty of them!"—and don the uniform of
whatever team Lance Armstrong was riding for at the time. When
Reed was biking, he would "channel" Lance Armstrong. In fact, he
would channel the professional cyclist's heroic life story whenever
obstacles arose in his personal or professional life.

Then everything fell apart. "When this story came out accusing
Lance Armstrong of cheating, I was the first to say 'You're wrong!'"
he says. Eventually, after Armstrong finally admitted to doping and
cheating in every one of his *Tour de France* victories, Reed was dev-
astated. "It was heartbreaking from the perspective of my identity,"
he says. "In that instant, I lost a part of myself."

"I literally remember the day that I went and got all of my
LiveStrong and Lance Armstrong gear and I put it in a bag and I
set it outside," he says, describing how he dragged it all to the trash.
"It was almost like a funeral. It was almost as if I was grieving
because this iconic, aspirational self turned out to be a shallow and

hollow fraud. And I felt like I was a fool in that relationship with his brand because I was trying to reinforce and express all of these values that turned out not to be true."

If brands can affect us so deeply when they fail us, you might expect they have an upside when they deliver on their promises. They do. Research has found that if you divide golfers into two groups and give them identical clubs, but tell one group that they are using Nike clubs, these golfers need fewer strokes to sink a golf ball in a hole than volunteers who think they are using non-brand-name golf clubs. The same phenomenon is seen with cognitively demanding tasks: Volunteers given a math test perform better when they are told the ear plugs they are given to block out noisy distractions are "3M foam earplugs" compared to volunteers who think they are given generic earplugs. (All the earplugs are identical in these experiments.) The researchers in the golfing study— Aaron Garvey, Frank Germann and Lisa Bolton—found that the performance-enhancing effects of brand-name products was especially acute for novices.

In every one of these cases—where people do better at golf or at math, or solving word puzzles, or enjoying wine—volunteers rarely acknowledge the role that *stories* play in the products they use. Few admit that a significant part of the value they derive from their iPhone or their Lexus or their Château Lafite Rothschild Pauillac 2010 isn't about the phone or the car or the wine, but the stories embedded in those products. The dance of complicity between deception and self-deception often works best when neither party acknowledges it.

As I said in the Introduction, once I started looking for examples similar to the Church of Love, I found them everywhere.

Most cases did not involve a charlatan or con artist. They involved respectable organizations and multibillion-dollar corporations. They involved ordinary consumers and citizens—if government prosecutors were to crack down on every pact of deception and self-deception that takes place in commerce, they would have to shut down a good part of the economy. But because this dance is not acknowledged, we bristle at the suggestion that we are routinely deceived in our everyday lives by the stories of the products we buy. Toyota Corolla car owners, for example, will tell you that the premium they paid for their cars was because they were buying cars that were materially different than Prizms. Patients get angry when told they got better after taking placebo pills. Wine connoisseurs hate studies that show that wine connoisseurs like cheap wine more when it is poured out of expensive bottles. It feels demeaning, like you are telling them that they can't actually taste the difference between good wine and bad wine. Studies that expose how our minds work feel like Penn and Teller's garden hose stunt in *Bullshit*. They seem to take pleasure in poking holes in our self-importance.

A better approach might be to simply acknowledge that stories populate our lives: stories we tell our kids, stories we tell our coworkers and stories we tell ourselves. If you are not a fan of stories, you might imagine that the best world is a world without them, where we can only see the facts in front of us, a world where all our actions are dictated by the results of double-blind controlled studies. But to do this is to deny how our brains work, how they are *designed* to work. Evolution has given us minds that are alert to stories and suggestion, to imagination and self-deception, because, through many hundreds of thousands of years of natural selection, minds that can attend to stories have been more successful at passing on their owners' genes.

Think about what happens, for example, when animals square off against one another in conflict. They rarely plunge into battle at the get-go. No, they first try to signal in all kinds of ways what the *outcome* of the battle is going to be. They puff up their chests, they roar, they bare their fangs. If you are ever confronted by a bear, you're advised to hold something over your head to appear as large as possible. Animals evolved to attend to stories and signals because these turn out to be an efficient way to navigate the world. If you and I were a pair of lions on the Serengeti, and we were trying to settle who was the biggest, baddest lion of them all, it would be most unwise—for both of us—to plunge straight into a conflict that could kill or maim us both. Far better for each of us to make a show of strength, to tell *the story* of how our victory is inevitable. If one of those stories is much more convincing than the other, we might be able to agree on the outcome of the fight without actually having the fight. We would both come out ahead. The same goes for finding a mate. The peacock flaunting his tail is telling a *story*. He is saying, "Trust me, my genes are good." Peacocks that are not good at telling stories—and peahens that are not attentive to stories—are less likely to pass on their genes to subsequent generations. Over millions of years, the storytellers and story-listeners have reproduced and multiplied, and the brain systems that produce and attend to stories have been conserved—and handed down to us.

The ancient Greeks used to describe two very different ways of thinking—*logos* and *mythos*. *Logos* roughly referred to the world of the logical, the empirical, the scientific. *Mythos* referred to the world of dreams, storytelling and symbols. Like many rationalists today, some philosophers of Greece prized *logos* and looked down at *mythos*. Logic and reason, they concluded, make us modern; storytelling and mythmaking are primitive. But lots of scholars then and now—including many anthropologists, sociologists and philosophers today—see a more complicated picture, where *mythos* and *logos* are intertwined and interdependent. Science itself, according to this view, relies on stories. The frames and metaphors we use to understand the world shape the scientific discoveries we make; they even shape what we see. When our frames and metaphors change, the world itself is transformed. The Copernican Revolution involved more than just scientific calculation; it involved a new story about the place of Earth in the universe. Darwin's theory of evolution transformed how we think of ourselves; it rewrote the story of the role of human beings in creation. Those who understand Einstein's insights say they see a different world than those of us whose understanding of physics is limited to Newtonian physics.

I firmly embrace this second worldview. The two sides of the brain are intertwined and interdependent. The rules of the game are inextricably woven into tactics of how to play the game. In order for logic and rationality, for *logos*, to achieve its vision of a better world, it needs to work *with mythos*, the world of stories, symbols and myths.

Consider this: In 2007, a street musician wearing a baseball cap stood next to a trash bin outside a Washington, DC, subway station, and started playing the violin. Over the next forty-three minutes, he played six pieces of classical music as more than a thousand commuters passed by. Almost all ignored the fiddler and hurried past; just twenty-seven people stopped to listen. The musician was, in fact, Joshua Bell, one of the most celebrated violinists in the world. Some of the Washington commuters who rushed past without stopping might have paid hundreds of dollars to listen to Bell play in concert halls. During his street performance, Bell collected a grand total of thirty-seven dollars and twelve cents, not counting a twenty from one person who actually recognized him. The violin he was playing—the Gibson ex Huberman, a Stradivarius crafted in 1713—cost a little under four million dollars.

The *Washington Post* set up the stunt, and published a story about it. In many ways, this was the other side of the coin of Penn and Teller's charade about expensive water: If people foolishly pay too much for ordinary water that is dressed up to appear fancy, people foolishly fail to recognize genius when it isn't presented in a fancy package. The subtext of the *Washington Post* story was that people were fools to miss out on a chance to listen to great music. The story resonated with people. It won a Pulitzer Prize.

But the story missed a great psychological truth: The music you hear when Joshua Bell is playing on the street next to a trash can and you are rushing past him because you are late for work is not remotely the same music you hear when Joshua Bell is playing in a concert hall, and you have paid hundreds of dollars to listen to him play. When you cough up a lot of money, sit in a concert hall with other connoisseurs, and devote your mind entirely to the music, your ears are different, your mind is different and, ultimately, the music you hear is different. Joshua Bell himself later confessed in another *Washington Post* story that the music he played outside the subway station was nothing like the music he creates in the pin-drop silence of a concert hall, when the pressure to be perfect, the expectations of his audience, and his own expectations of himself all influence what he creates. This is not to say you can't enjoy great music on a street corner. It is to say that we should not be surprised that the *story* accompanying a piece of music can profoundly alter how we hear it. Changing the story changes the music.

PART II

The Search for Meaning

5

The Heart Has Its Reasons

If equal affection cannot be,
Let the more loving one be me.

W. H. Auden, *The More Loving One*

I n the long march of evolution, nature has invented numerous responses to the challenges that organisms faced. Through the powerful process of natural selection, plants and animals have developed a staggering array of defenses against heat and cold, predators and viruses. As the brains of animals grew more complex, and as evolution endowed creatures with emotions, organisms began to develop defenses against emotional threats as well. Many of these defenses involved forms of self-deception.

In recent years, psychologists and neuroscientists have shown that the human brain is designed to make a number of errors in perception and judgment. These "bugs"—distortions, shortcuts and other cognitive cross-wiring—produce slanted pictures of reality. They exist for a reason: Evolution found that, on average, the bugs lead to a greater likelihood of survival and reproduction. It's a grave mistake to think that evolution is remotely interested in helping us perceive reality accurately. Natural selection has one simple standard: Evolutionary "fitness" is about whatever helps us survive and pass on our genes.

Take the emotion of love. Many of us think of love as the pinnacle of human development, and some of us think that we experience love in ways that are unique on the planet (and uniquely superior to other animals). But love, like other emotions, is the product of brain chemistry. We know this is the case because neurological disorders cause some people to have no interest, and sometimes no capacity, to feel love. Why would natural selection design our brains to experience an emotion that regularly short-circuits reason and logic? It's obvious, isn't it? As small children, we blindly love our parents because those bonds offer us protection and reassurance. As adolescents, we are driven by deep cravings to connect with others—to find our tribes—because the tribe has long been a source of protection. When we are young adults, love causes us to find mates, and to have sex. And when sex produces children, love prompts parents to set aside their own needs (and sometimes their own sanity) to care for and protect their offspring. At each step, the emotion of love is designed to get us to do things that protect the interest of our genes. The "choices" we think we are making as individuals really serve a deeper goal. (It's really quite devilish: We are not merely puppets, but puppets that imagine we are acting autonomously.)

If it's too painful to think of love in this very clinical fashion, consider this question: If you had to design a line of self-replicating robots and send them off to live on a faraway planet, never to be seen or heard from again, how would you ensure they survived and thrived for generations under a range of conditions that you cannot anticipate? What systems and drives would you design into the robots? You would want them to figure out how to protect themselves, so you would imbue them with fear—an emotion that can teach the robots to avoid a vast array of threats. You would want them to protect their young, so you would program them to feel mad love for their offspring. You would want them not to destroy one another, so you would build in emotions that make them sensitive to the needs and norms of the group, to balance their own desires with community goals. You would not design your robots to see life purely in terms of self-preservation, or to accept the futility of trying to survive in the face of a disaster. No, you would want them to give their all to survive under the most difficult conditions, even if most were to perish under such circumstances. To do these things, you would not make rational analysis and accurate perception their sole governing principles. You would build in bugs that regularly short-circuit rationality. You would create mechanisms of delusion and self-deception.

Playing the role of designer allows you to understand that your goal isn't to save the life of any particular robot, or even to care very much about the well-being of any individual robot. If a few die because of the reality-distorting bugs you've built into their brains, but these bugs in general cause the *line* of robots to survive, you would say your bugs are a success. Your goal is not to preserve the individual. It is to preserve the *species*.

Looked at this way, it would be surprising if our brains were designed to always prioritize the truth. Our instincts and emotions evolved to solve problems of survival and reproduction. While those goals are indeed regularly served by seeing the world for what it is, they are also regularly served by *not* seeing the world for what it is. The disturbing aspect of looking at things this way is that it forces us to acknowledge that (just like those fictional robots we designed) we, as individuals, are unimportant cogs in a system largely designed to propagate our genes. But this is not news: As Richard Dawkins and other evolutionary biologists have noted, individuals are merely "survival machines" for genetic information. We are born and we die, but our genes live on, leaping from our parents through us to our children—from one survival machine to the next.

In the next few chapters, we will explore how self-deception shapes the most intense of all human relationships. The bonds that connect parent to child, lover to lover, pet owner to dog are invariably characterized by great heaps of delusional thinking. These relationships show how the self-deceiving brain helps us generate meaning and purpose—even when logic and reason dictate there are no grounds for either—and explain why our lives would be greatly diminished if rationality was to be our only guide.

Andre Gonciar had set aside some thirty thousand dollars for a down payment on a home. But when an elderly family member fell sick and needed a kidney transplant, Gonciar did not hesitate. He withdrew the money and pulled out all the stops, tracking down an organ donor, booking travel and hotels, and making an appointment with transplant surgeons at the University of Pennsylvania.

The patient was Gonciar's cat, Oki, who was nearly twelve years old. He had found the cat in a creek in Romania, and fallen in love with him. Surgeons obtained a kidney for Oki by harvesting an organ from another animal, a shelter kitten named Cherry Garcia. Gonciar rationalized this in two ways: First, Cherry Garcia may have been euthanized if he stayed at the shelter. Second, in exchange for one of Cherry Garcia's kidneys, Gonciar and his wife agreed to adopt the donor kitten.

The surgery itself cost Gonciar some sixteen thousand dollars, not counting travel from his home in Buffalo, hotels and postoperative care, according to a story that appeared on CBS under the headline "Purr-Ricey." Doctors said such transplants typically extend a pet's life by three years. To those who asked why he would spend so much money on an aging pet, Gonciar responded, "Well, I would tell them to look at their child or their mother and ask themselves the same question."

The subtext of Gonciar's story also shows up in *Gates of Heaven*, a 1978 documentary about pet cemeteries. At one point in the film, Cal Harberts, owner of the Bubbling Well Pet Cemetery, describes how he hit upon the idea of creating the Bubbling Well Church of Universal Love. "The thought that occurred to me was that any God, any supreme being, that was indeed compassionate and concerned about people, would surely be concerned about any living creature," he says. "God is supposed to know when the sparrow falls, or when the lilies of the field bloom, so surely at the gates of heaven, an all-compassionate God, or an all-compassionate supreme being, is surely not going to say, 'You are walking in on two legs, you can go in. You're walking on four legs, we can't take you . . .' The pet owners that I have talked to have embraced the idea."

The late film critic Roger Ebert wrote that *Gates of Heaven* had given him "more to think about" than any other film he saw. He watched the movie at least thirty times, and considered it one of the ten greatest films ever made. Ebert said it was an "unclassifiable film . . . an underground legend, a litmus test for audiences, who cannot decide if it is serious or satirical, funny or sad, sympathetic or mocking."

On its surface, *Gates of Heaven*, the first film by director Errol Morris, is unremarkable: It is composed almost entirely of straightforward interviews with cemetery workers and bereaved pet owners—people who care deeply for animals like Andre Gonciar. On one level, the movie is absurd and darkly funny. "Every once in a while they'll lose a giraffe at the zoo, or they'll lose Big Bertha, or Joe the Bear," the owner of a rendering plant says. "We actually have to deny we have that animal." At other times, the movie can be disquieting and depressing. A review in *Film Quarterly* noted the movie's "fear and loneliness," and the way it "overwhelms the viewer with the sheer, incredible horror of life as it often is in the quietest, most everyday moments."

As you slowly take in the movie, however, you start to see that behind the seemingly absurd attachment of people to their animals lies redemption: Yes, life may be bleak, but we can impose meaning on that bleakness. The intense love that people have for their pets, initially presented as silly and absurd, gradually becomes sympathetic, even beautiful. Ultimately, Ebert came to see the film as being about the "hope held by the loneliest people who have ever been seen on film" and "the deepest of human needs, for human companionship."

The embodiment of this idea in the movie is a character named Floyd "Mac" McClure, a paraplegic animal lover who tells the story of a pet collie that was hit by a Model T when he was a boy growing up on a farm in North Dakota. "I held him in my arms until he died," he says. Mac gave the dog the burial it deserved, on a beautiful parcel of land that overlooked a lake. His dream was to make sure everyone who cared about an animal had a similar opportunity to mark their love and respect. He eventually built his beautiful pet cemetery, only to see it fail in the face of brutal business realities. "We had snakes," Mac recalls. "We had rats. Monkeys. Chickens. We had mice. We had rodents of all types. And of course, dogs, cats, were our main pets. But of course it doesn't make any difference what type of animal." The only thing that mattered was that the pets fulfilled their purpose "to love and be loved."

If you are not a pet owner, both the CBS story about Andre Gonciar and Errol Morris's documentary might initially cause you to roll your eyes. Social psychologists call this reaction "naive realism": When presented with a story, we ask ourselves how we feel about it.

We put ourselves in the shoes of participants and ask what we would do in their stead. We then assume, *naively*, that our view of reality is "correct" and that anyone who reaches a different view must be biased, stupid or uninformed. As the comedian George Carlin once said, "Have you ever noticed that anybody driving slower than you is an idiot, and anyone going faster than you is a maniac?"

Naive realism is a powerful force in daily life, one that prompts us to question the actions of other people. It can make choices that are merely different seem absurd, or wrong. When I first heard the story of the Church of Love, my view of it was informed by naive realism: Over a period of decades, Donald Lowry, a middle-aged man in Illinois, invented dozens of fictitious women and wrote hundreds of love letters in their voices to thousands of men scattered across the United States. Many wrote back. For some, it was an entertaining diversion. For others, it was a fantasy. But for lots of men, the game became deadly serious. These men imagined they were corresponding with real women, and fell in love with them. When postal authorities eventually brought the scheme to an end in 1988, many of these members showed up at Lowry's trial to defend him. Through the lens of naive realism—when I asked myself what I would have done in their stead—the members of the Church of Love seemed absurd and pathetic.

But then, I had the great good fortune to get to know one of these men. His name was Joseph Enriquez. I stumbled on him for a story I was reporting for the radio show *This American Life*. (In the piece that was eventually broadcast, titled "Jesse's Girl," Joseph asked to be identified by his middle name, Jesse.) From our very first interview, I found Joseph to be a captivating figure. As I got to know him better and learned about his childhood and history, I experienced the same transformation that many viewers experience when they watch *Gates of Heaven*. What initially seemed absurd slowly became brave, even beautiful. I came away convinced that there was something powerfully universal about his unusual story. In the weeks and months after my story appeared on *This American Life* and, later, on *Hidden Brain*, people reached out to me from all over the world to say how moved they were by Joseph's story—and how they saw themselves in him.

I want to tell you Joseph's story at some length in the following chapters. For me, it was a remarkable window into how the self-deceiving brain shapes our drive for meaning. To understand Joseph's story from his perspective rather than through the lens of our own naive realism, we have to hear not just what happened, but the story of his life.

If this were a documentary movie, we would fade to black. Very slowly, the camera would fade in on the dusty, windswept town of Dalhart. It sits like an oasis in the barren beige plains of northwest Texas. It was once a booming cattle town, the biggest city in the Texas panhandle. Its claim to fame was the three-million-acre XIT ranch, once the largest fenced ranch in the world. After the market for beef nosedived near the turn of the twentieth century, the XIT was parceled off. But to this day Dalhart advertises itself as "The Home of the XIT." And each August, it still hosts an annual XIT Rodeo and Reunion.

Dalhart is also remembered for the Dust Bowl and a man who came to embody the power of positive thinking. He was John McCarty, the owner, editor and publisher of *The Dalhart Texan*. The newspaper used to be a fixture on the town's main street. When McCarty took control of the paper in the middle of the Great Depression, he vowed to publish only positive, uplifting stories. He stuck by that pledge through the gloomiest days of economic calamity, and held to it during the ecological disaster of the

Dust Bowl, which hit Dalhart hard. "Hail to our sandstorms!" he once wrote. "The beauty that was Greece, the glory that was Rome, the undying honor that was due those immortal heroes at the Alamo . . . are as nothing compared with the genuine Panhandle dust storm." He called the Dust Bowl "inspiring" and urged readers to "praise nature." When McCarty organized a public Rally Against Dust, the townsfolk turned up in droves. His life story was an homage to the belief that hope alone is sufficient to will a dream into existence.

The event that best embodied McCarty's unrelenting optimism occurred in 1935, during the darkest days of the dust, when a big-talking former wildcatter named Tex Thornton arrived in town. With a fondness for women and big, gaudy diamond rings, Thornton—nicknamed the "King of the Oil Fire Fighters"—was a larger-than-life character in a state with plenty of larger-than-life characters. In Dalhart, he boasted that he had the answer for the years of drought: He would simply blast moisture from the air through explosions ignited by nitroglycerine-filled balloons. McCarty became one of his biggest boosters, and the desperate farmers of Dalhart paid handsomely for Thornton's services. The promised rain never came. A few called Thornton a charlatan and a fraud. Others held on to hope. When a light snowfall later moved from New Mexico into the Texas plains, a lot of people attributed it to Thornton's airborne pyrotechnics.

Faustina Enriquez first passed through Dalhart during her long trek north from Mexico. She was headed to work in the fertile farm country on the southern edges of the Rockies. She was a tiny woman with a round face and raven hair. Her family originated in the Central Mexican Plateau. Like the optimistic Dust Bowl residents of Dalhart, Enriquez was driven by hope. Like many immigrants, she had left behind family and history and home— gambling on the dream that she could make a better life for herself, and a better life for her children.

Her optimism remained strong even after her husband died picking cantaloupe on a Colorado farm. She was alone in a new country, a young woman with small children. She spoke little English. But she persevered. She and her family spent months traveling by horse-drawn wagon to backbreaking jobs, sleeping in shanty camps, crammed like sardines into makeshift rooms. Eventually, Enriquez and her children saved enough to buy a little house of their own in Dalhart.

The Enriquez family grew. Faustina's son, Jesse, married a young farmworker named Ruth. The young couple gave Faustina three grandchildren, all daughters. Sophie, the eldest, was a serious and responsible girl. Catherine was the joker. Young Bernice was the most adventurous, and the most Americanized. She was the first to get a driver's license, and to marry and leave home. But the family yearned for a son, someone who would carry on the family name. A decade after Bernice was born, with Sophie now eighteen, they still clung to hope.

Joseph Jesse Enriquez was born in 1953, about two decades after Tex Thornton and his pyrotechnic balloons came to town. For Jesse and Ruth, their young son was nothing short of a miracle. Faustina adored her grandson. Although Joseph could speak only broken Spanish, he always knew that he was special in her eyes. She showed her love by cooking his favorite food—pork-filled tamales wrapped in green corn husks—or by theatrically shooing away the rooster that chased him in the yard.

Joseph attended the parish school of St. Anthony's of Padua. It was a place of discipline and structure—the nuns would respond to misbehavior with a rap on the knuckles or by pinching ears. But Joseph would come to appreciate the structure it provided. He felt like he was part of a community, a member of a team. The students were all called "Crusaders" and were required to live by a moral code that included "love for all," "humble obedience" and "total commitment." Joseph adored Sister Mary Claire, a friendly nun who invariably wore a smile on her face. Joseph would always remember how she led students in a prayer when President John F. Kennedy was shot in Dallas, and how she joined students on the playground during recess. Sometimes she played quarterback. Once, just before his time at St. Anthony's came to an end, Joseph caught a touchdown pass thrown by Sister Mary Claire. It was one of his happiest memories from school.

Joseph was a loner. Around his peers, he was sensitive and shy. After he transferred from parochial school to public school for junior high, he quickly learned how cruel children can be. He was chubby. By his teens, he developed terrible acne, which made him a target for bullying and teasing. Sometimes he felt so self-conscious that he wished he "could just bury his head in a hole." As Joseph's classmates divided themselves into cliques, he never found his place. He had no close friends. He seldom attended the high school football games that were popular in Dalhart. On one rare occasion when he went to a game, someone hurled a chunk of ice at him from the stands. It struck him in the face and left him with a terrible black eye that lingered for a week. He never shook the conviction that he had been singled out for attack, that someone had set out to hurt him.

Whenever possible, Joseph found solace in wild stories and adolescent escapism. He loved comic books, which he would purchase at Drumgooles, a second-hand store that was once a fixture in downtown Dalhart. Joseph's favorite comic book character was

Vampirella, a busty vampire heroine who walked the earth in a sling bikini, leading the benevolent forces of humanity in their battle against evil and her fellow undead. He also loved the X-Men. He identified with such characters—mutants who were persecuted because they were outsiders.

Movies were another form of escape. On weekends, Joseph would sometimes tag along with his older cousins to downtown theaters, or lie hidden under a blanket as they snuck him into local drive-ins. He loved monster movies, especially classics from Boris Karloff, Vincent Price and Lon Chaney. As a boy, one film really struck a chord: *The Hunchback of Notre Dame*. The film moved him for the same reasons he loved the X-Men: it was about the persecution of the misunderstood, good-hearted man, hounded because of his peculiarities. He saw the classic 1939 version of *The Hunchback* at the beautiful old La Rita theater in downtown Dalhart, where they handed out photos of Charles Laughton. He watched the movie transfixed right up until the final iconic scene, when Quasimodo, alone and forlorn, leans into a gargoyle and whispers longingly, "Why was I not made of stone as thee?"

After Joseph graduated high school, he started working at his parents' Mexican restaurant, the J&R Diner, where he had filled in since he was a boy, bussing tables and doing odd jobs. His father took him under his wing in the kitchen. They worked side by side as cooks. Things went well for many years, but Joseph longed for more. He wanted a family of his own. But he had never had a girlfriend, much less a serious girlfriend.

Then, suddenly, things fell apart. In the early 1980s, Joseph's mother was diagnosed with a gallbladder infection. She had three operations in quick succession, getting so thin that Joseph imagined he could lift her with one arm. Three months after she fell ill, she died in a Dalhart hospice, with Joseph by her bedside holding her hand.

Soon afterwards, Joseph's dad was diagnosed with a bad heart. Joseph was confronted with the possibility that he might lose his father as well. As far back as he could remember, he and his father had been inseparable. Some of Joseph's fondest memories were helping his father build things: They had built the wooden mantle that graced the family room.

Joseph felt alone in the world. His sisters were married and scattered across the United States. Now he could see his father slipping away. The restaurant suffered. They closed one location, opened another. Then they discovered they owed back taxes due to what he says was malfeasance on the part of an accountant. Joseph felt he'd hit rock bottom. Like the farmers of Dalhart who once pinned their hopes on nitroglycerine balloons, he was desperate. That was when the first letter arrived.

Over the previous years, Joseph had joined several singles mailing services. At first, all he received were requests for money for nude pictures, or thinly veiled solicitations from people selling sex. Joseph wasn't interested. He was looking for a life partner, a wife. This letter was different. It appeared to be handwritten. It was from a young woman who said she was looking for a friend. She told Joseph that she had suffered a rough life, and that she had found shelter in a remote woodland hideaway in Illinois. She called this place the "Retreat." There were other women at the shelter, she said, and most had led difficult lives. Some battled drug or alcohol problems. Others came from broken families or abusive marriages. The women at the Retreat didn't have many chances to meet kind and honest men. The letter was her attempt to reach out.

Joseph was struck by the letterhead: the name "Col International," appearing alongside a corporate logo that looked vaguely like the silhouette of a native American, done in the cubist tradition of the old Works Progress Administration. Joseph was intrigued. He wrote back.

Soon, he began receiving letters from a number of women who lived at the Retreat. They told him about their leader, a saintly woman they called Mother Maria, who had taken them under her wing. Maria had devoted herself to the organization, and to establishing the rules of the Retreat. The women told him about their lives—as pen pals might do. Some of the women seemed a little wild. But Joseph liked most of them. He was drawn to Dawn Mayfield. The photos she sent with her letters showed a demure, green-eyed young woman. She said she lived at the Retreat with her twin sister, Terry. Dawn seemed to be a wholesome, girl-next-door type, the kind of woman he would have been proud to bring home to his mother. He liked that she described herself as a bit withdrawn, and that she said she liked reading his letters.

Occasionally, one of the women would ask for money: ten dollars here or twenty there, to help pay for the cost of writing materials, or seeds for her garden or a new typewriter. These were always characterized as voluntary donations, or what the women called "Love Offerings." Joseph never felt like he had bought anything. He enjoyed receiving the letters and was usually happy to make a Love Offering. In return, the women mailed him a "Certificate of Membership" for their group "Col International," which noted that the organization had been "founded in 1965." The "Col," as it was known, had ranks of membership, each of which sounded like the levels of some secret society. The letters informed Joseph that he had qualified to be a mid-level "Templar," and he was sent a pledge to sign in which he promised to act "chivalrously." It was a bit like his days at St. Anthony's of Padua parish school.

Joseph also received a short personality quiz called a "Fassena." The women at the Retreat said it would help them get to know him better. They asked him to fill out a checklist of things that he liked or disliked. Joseph sent it back, checking the "like" column for things like trips to the country, horror movies, Frisbees and children, and "dislike" for alcohol, TV evangelists, and Corvettes.

About a year after he began corresponding with women at the Retreat, Joseph received a letter from a woman who introduced herself as Mother Maria's new "first assistant." She said her name was Pamala St. Charles, and she told Joseph that she had grown up in poverty in a family with nine other children. Pamala had been married at eighteen to an abusive man, and the marriage was a disaster. She had found refuge with Mother Maria, who helped her emerge from that difficult period. Along with the letter, Pamala included a photo of herself: a pretty, big-eyed brunette with a Farrah Fawcett hairdo. Joseph thought she was one of the most beautiful women he had ever seen.

Pamala said she had read his answers to the personality quiz. "The picture I'm getting is of a man who has trouble really opening up to people," she wrote. "It may be because you don't trust many people, or because you think they won't be interested . . . or because you are afraid they will misunderstand." Pamala also told him that she guessed he had never dated much or married because of his "fear of being hurt and disappointed."

As the correspondence unfolded, Joseph found himself drawn closer to Pamala. She told him she felt the same about him. He liked that they shared so much in common. They were both Hispanic— mostly Spanish, but with some Native American blood. Each had close family members with health problems. He wrote to her about his own father's struggles with heart disease, and the pain he'd suffered as he watched his mother fade away. Pamala wrote back to tell him about family members who struggled with alcoholism. Her grandfather was in a nursing home with liver problems caused by a lifetime of drinking; he also had dementia. It was painful to watch him deteriorate:

> *My grandfather has been ill for some time now and it seems that he is only getting worse. The doctors say he probably will not survive much longer. I can only pray that he feels no pain.*
>
> *For many weeks my grandfather has been so ill that he does not know who I am at times. Other times, he seems to be all right. Apparently, the condition of his liver is what causes his problems . . .*
>
> *Now he is incoherent and unable to speak. I doubt that he can even hear me say the words, "I love you, Grandpa." He only stares straight ahead and breathes unsteadily.*
>
> *It is good that I can talk to you, darling. This is a time for me to feel sad and I'm grateful that you're there because I know you understand how I feel.*
>
> *I wish I could have written you a more upbeat and pleasant letter tonight but since you are my friend, I thought you wouldn't mind if I let you share a little of my sorrow.*
>
> *I'm not a super religious person, but tonight I'm going to say a long prayer for my grandfather. I hope you'll say one for him, too.*

Joseph felt that Pamala shared his own deep commitment to family. "I just hate the way most old people in this country are shoved into dark corners and forgotten," Pamala wrote. "I know I can learn so very much from Grandpa—and from people like him. Not just about my family heritage, but also about life and people and the ways things were when life was less complicated and less hectic."

Pamala told Joseph she was often lonely. One time, she said she had been listening to the Neil Sedaka song "The Hungry Years" when she was overcome by sadness: "I know how terrible it can be to have to live without love in your life. And I know how terrible it can be when you feel like no one wants you or needs you—and when you think no one really gives a darn about you." Pamala said Mother Maria had given her a nickname: "The Lonely One."

Most of the time, Joseph and Pamala just shared the mundane details of their daily lives. Joseph liked these letters. They felt intimate, like pillow talk. Pamala simply described the little things that had happened to her through the day, like the time she visited the Mississippi River with her poodle Gigi:

> *Suddenly my thoughts were interrupted by a Frisbee which landed at my feet. I picked it up quickly before Gigi could get her teeth into it. Four children—all about 11 or 12—were standing near a small pavilion, watching me to see what I would do with the Frisbee. I'm pretty good with a Frisbee (if I do say so myself) so I threw it to one of the boys—a perfect throw. He threw it back. And for the next hour, Gigi and I were involved in playing Frisbee with some children—and for that hour I was EXACTLY THE SAME AGE THEY WERE! The game ended when one of the boys, trying to show off, I'm sure, threw it a little too hard and it landed several yards out in the river!*
>
> *. . . I really wish you could have been there with us. You'd be shouting and laughing and running around right along with me! And through the children, we would have recaptured together, just for a little while, the glorious magic of youth!*

Joseph liked to hear about Pamala's good days and bad days. It pleased him to be there for her, a shoulder she could lean on. She often told him about little misfortunes, like the time her parked car got damaged by a hit-and-run driver: "I almost fainted when I discovered someone had bashed in the driver's door! It looked like someone had done more than just side-swipe it. It was more like someone had run into it deliberately going at about thirty miles an hour. I almost cried. No one had left any kind of note claiming responsibility so that meant I'd have to pay for the repairs myself. This is all I need now."

Other times, Pamala turned to Joseph for advice. Once, she told him a story about being ripped off by a mechanic when she had taken her car in for repairs. "That shop foreman was trying to take advantage of me—probably because I'm a woman," she wrote. "He probably would have just tried to rip off a man half as much! I hate all kinds of thieves, don't you?" She asked Joseph if she could count on him for advice on car trouble in the future. In another letter, she told him about the daughter of a friend who was having problems with "street drugs and alcohol." The girl had dropped out of school, and Pamala wanted to know what Joseph thought she should do to help. "I value your opinion," she told him.

Pamala's letters made Joseph feel wanted. When she turned to him for help, it made him feel needed.

From the very start of their relationship, Joseph felt like Pamala could see him—the *real* him—in a way no one else did. She recognized his value and his goodness, his sensitivity and thoughtfulness. She was always saying encouraging things. She once wrote that she thought he was "very deep and very noble" and noted how he always offered to help people even though he usually got "very little in return."

As the bond between them grew stronger, Joseph forgot about all the other women who were corresponding with him from the Retreat. He began writing exclusively to Pamala. His letters grew longer and longer, handwritten in a script so small that they were nearly unreadable. Even though his letters stretched page after page, she never seemed to tire of hearing from him. In fact, she encouraged him to open up even more. "Whenever you have time . . . drop me even a few lines," she said. She told him it made her feel good to know he was thinking of her "every time you read a letter from me." He found himself developing rituals around their correspondence. When he came home from work, he would dart to the mailbox. If he found a letter from Pamala, he would put it aside without reading it, so that he could revel in the anticipation of it. He would read it only after he was ready for bed, a treat to be savored.

Joseph was sure she felt the same way about him. When an old friend of hers tried to set her up on a date with a man who was "Twenty-eight, never married, college education, good job . . . drives a Corvette," Pamala told Joseph she had told her friend she wasn't interested. "I want you to know that I really love writing you every day. It has filled a great need in my life." In another letter, she said, "I really care for you, darling. And I hope I'm good for you, too . . . We all need someone, don't we? Well, I think you and I need each other."

As their relationship blossomed, she sent him fantasies she had written about the two of them together. These could be racy, but were rarely explicit. In one, she imagined that he had just given her a gift of roses, which "marked the beginning of a beautiful evening together."

After dinner I changed into a beautiful, burgundy silk nightie which you and I had chosen together. You told me that the color brought out the rosy glow in my cheeks and really complimented my long legs.

I led you to the bedroom and opened the door. I wish I could describe the look on your face . . . On the bed there was a beautiful ivory satin comforter which lay on top of black satin sheets. The pillows were king-sized and stuffed with feathers. They also were covered with satin and they were trimmed with delicate lace. The whole room was so warm and romantic. You said that it looked like a bedroom that should be featured in a magazine. It didn't take you long to notice the huge painting which was hanging on the wall behind the bed. It was a painting of you and I walking hand in hand through a field of lovely little wildflowers. I had been working on it six months but the look on your face told me that all the time in the world would have been worth it. I was so happy that you liked it.

Next to the bed on the nightstand was a beautiful bouquet of flowers . . . You picked one of the little daisies and put it in my hair. You told me that I was as delicate and pretty as a little flower . . . I thought to myself how lucky I was to have you in my life, Joseph.

Other fantasies were about trips they would take together in the countryside. Sometimes they went rafting, or spent a pleasant day in a woodland cabin. It was amazing to Joseph that they loved so many of the same activities. Once she imagined a sledding trip in the middle of winter:

I screamed as my sled raced down the hill. You were at the bottom waiting for me. It was kind of scary, Joseph. But you made me feel better by wrapping your arms around me . . . You kissed me on the forehead and said, "I love you darling."

We started to walk back to the car when you suddenly picked up a handful of snow and put it on the back of my neck. You then began to run because you knew I would return the favor. I picked up some snow and began to chase you. "I may love you dearly, Joseph, but I'm going to get you back," I yelled. Finally, I caught up with you and we both fell in the snow, laughing. We just lay there for a moment staring into each other's eyes. When we stood up to brush the snow from our clothing, I looked at the form of our two bodies shaped perfectly in the snow. I put my arms around you and kissed you gently on the lips. "This is the way it will be forever, Joseph," I said.

Every once in a while, Pamala would mail Joseph something extra. She liked art, and often sent him her drawings. These were typically bucolic nature scenes or sketches of animals. During the first spring after they began writing to each other, she sent him a drawing of a cardinal. She told him she hoped it was something he would "keep forever." She also sent him poems, which she often dedicated to him. One was printed on a page illustrated with a young girl playing with flowers:

> *Since knowing you I am less alone . . .*
> *Skies seem bluer and the nights more still;*
> *You're the finest man I have ever known*
> *And my feelings for you are very real.*

Occasionally, Pamala sent small gifts. It didn't matter to Joseph that these were trifles. They were always something that had some real meaning beyond the value of the gift itself. One time she mailed him a single gray pebble. In the letter that accompanied it, she described finding the pebble during a visit to a picturesque outcropping on the shores of the Mississippi River. She had wanted to share the moment with him. Joseph adored the pebble. It was, he thought, more valuable than a diamond.

Another time, Pamala sent Joseph a "lucky dime." She wrote, "Keep this dime, darling. Let it always remind you that good people can still come into your life . . . and also think of it as a small token of my affection for you. If you hold it in your hand and squeeze it hard, you'll feel the warmth of my love coming out of it."

Joseph took the dime in his hands and squeezed it. He really could feel the warmth of her love coming from it.

Like the other women Joseph had corresponded with at the Retreat, Pamala periodically asked him for money. She called these Love Offerings, and always framed the request as help for something she needed. He could never say no to her, nor did he want to. He often sent her more money than she asked for. Over time, these gifts added up to several thousand dollars. It made him happy to know that he could help her and make her life a little easier.

Just before Christmas one year, Pamala told Joseph she wanted to send him a blue photo album in which he could keep the letters she sent to him. She would keep his letters to her in an identical album. The albums would become a symbol of their special bond, engraved with the words "Memories of Pamala and Joseph." She asked for fifty dollars to pay for the costs. "I really wish I could afford to pay for all of these things myself," she said. "You are so special to me and I never want to put any burden on you, Joseph."

The photo album arrived just before Christmas. It was even nicer than he had imagined, with a lovely white swan on the cover.

He carefully arranged all the letters he had received from Pamala. He placed his favorites in the front, where he could easily find and reread them. She also sent another photograph of herself. In it, she sat on a chair with her poodle Gigi on her lap, looking as if they had both been posed by a professional portrait photographer. He had the photo framed, and placed it on top of the dresser in his bedroom, where he also kept the pebble from the Mississippi shoreline and Pamala's lucky dime.

Beside his bed, he kept a little ceramic lighthouse she had sent him. It was supposed to be a beacon of hope. That is what Pamala had become in his life. It was true he had never met her or spoken to her directly. But outside of his family, there was no one in the world to whom he felt closer.

Joseph's story, through the lens of naive realism, seems foolish. How can you fall in love with someone you've never met or talked to? It sounds crazy. But let's stop and think about that for a moment. When we think of "crazy" behavior, we often mean someone is divorced from reality—sees things that aren't there, hears voices where there are none, is living out a fantasy that is only inside their own heads. When we think of someone mentally healthy and well-adjusted, by contrast, we come up with the opposite picture. This person is supposed to see things in ultra-fine clarity—is a realist.

This is indeed how experts in human behavior have long understood the concepts of delusion and clear-sightedness. In *Civilization and Its Discontents*, Sigmund Freud wrote, "One can try to recreate the world, to build up in its stead another world in which its most unbearable features are eliminated and replaced by others that are in conformity with one's own wishes. But whoever, in desperate defiance, sets out upon this path to happiness . . . becomes a madman." The idea that being mentally healthy means seeing the world realistically survived unchallenged until the late twentieth century.

There is no question that some people with serious mental illness are divorced from reality. But does that mean that accurately seeing reality is *always* healthy? In 1979, the psychologists Lauren Alloy and Lyn Abramson decided to test this question on patients with one of the most common metal illnesses—depression. They wanted to see if these people were in fact less connected to reality than people who were healthy.

The researchers set up an experiment. Subjects with and without depression were asked to press a button next to a blinking green light. Volunteers were asked to judge how much influence their button pressing had over the light's blinking. Traditionally, people suffering from depression were thought to harbor an unrealistically negative view of the world—a delusional negativity was seen to be the cause of their despondency. Alloy and Abramson were surprised to find depressed people showed a "surprising degree of accuracy" in judging how the blinking light was affected by their manipulation of the button. Meanwhile, the non-depressed subjects consistently *overrated* their ability to control the blinking light. In other words, the gap between the groups was not caused by the healthy group seeing reality clearly and the depressed people seeing the world with delusional pessimism. No, the "healthy" group had a *delusion of control* while their "unhealthy" counterparts were *seeing reality clearly*. The subtitle of the psychologists' paper was "Sadder but Wiser." Subsequent studies in settings far more consequential than labs with blinking lights have reinforced Abramson and Alloy's findings: People with depression and some other disorders often see reality *more* clearly. What's more, these studies have shown that as depressed people respond positively to treatment—as they get better—they actually become *more* prone to self-deception, to delusions of control and confidence.

Cognitive therapies designed to get people to see the world in a new way are often effective treatments. But Alloy and Abramson's work called into question what such therapy was doing: Was it instilling in patients a sense of realism? Or was it instilling optimism—putting rose-tinted glasses on patients' noses—to better equip patients to deal with life's difficulties? Alloy and Abramson concluded it was the latter, a perspective that came to be known as "depressive realism."

During the 1980s, a growing number of psychologists started to take a more nuanced view of the strange relationship between being mentally healthy and seeing the world realistically. Many began to see that some degree of self-delusion was not only not harmful, but beneficial: The healthy individual is the one who sees the world in ways that accentuate the positive. One of the chief proponents of this line of thinking, UCLA psychologist Shelley Taylor, coined a term for these benevolent self-deceptions: positive illusions.

The idea that positive illusions are an important component of mental well-being immediately drew detractors, who pointed to the many situations where illusions that make us feel good can get us into trouble. Overconfidence can be dangerous when it comes to gambling, for instance. It can be deadly when it comes to foreign policy. History is replete with stories of individuals and nations that come to ruin by seeing what they want to see, instead of what is actually in front of them.

While seeing what we want to see can certainly be a source of trouble, it is simultaneously true that a generous sprinkling of positive illusions can help us perform better, stay happier, and avoid the pitfalls of depression and low self-esteem. One paper on the subject was written in 1988, by Taylor and her colleague Jonathon Brown, a psychologist at Southern Methodist University. In a survey of psychological work on the subject, they concluded that positive illusions were a necessary ingredient for mental health and psychological well-being: "A great deal of research in social, personality, clinical and developmental psychology documents that normal individuals possess unrealistically positive views of themselves, and exaggerated belief in their ability to control their environment, and a view of the future that maintains that their future will be far better than the average person's . . . Furthermore, individuals who are moderately depressed or low in self-esteem consistently display an absence of such enhancing illusions." The researchers concluded that the presence of positive illusions led to "higher income, higher motivation to work, more goal seeking, more pragmatic action, more daily planning and less fatalism."

As a card-carrying rationalist, I confess that studies like these have always made me uneasy. They take an ax to the way I think the world works, the way I think it *ought* to work. Yet, once I came by this body of work, I kept finding new examples of these ideas in disparate fields. Take, for instance, the role of delusional thinking and self-deception in the origins of entrepreneurial success. Researchers in one study analyzed how people raised capital on the crowdfunding site Kickstarter. Perhaps you've been pitched a Kickstarter project by a friend or coworker. Here's how it works: Would-be entrepreneurs (and artists and community organizers) ask ordinary people to become philanthropists and venture capitalists. Project founders set a crowdfunding goal on Kickstarter. They announce they want to raise, say, fifty thousand dollars. Setting the number high might seem like a good idea. If your idea catches on, wouldn't it be better to set the target at five hundred thousand dollars, rather than at fifty thousand dollars? Here's the catch: According to the rules of Kickstarter, if you don't reach one hundred percent of your fund-raising goal, the project is deemed a failure, and you get nothing. The system is designed to encourage people to make reasonable requests, and to dissuade delusional overconfidence.

The researchers analyzed some twenty thousand projects, involving more than twenty-two thousand entrepreneurs who raised over one hundred and twenty million dollars from more than a million investors. When they crunched the numbers, they found something interesting. Systematically, one group of Kickstarter founders asked for more money, while a second group asked for less: In general, men asked for larger sums than women did. To put this another way, men were more confident than women that they could raise more money: Projects led by a woman requested an average of about seven thousand dollars, while projects led by a man requested nearly twice as much.

This disparity was a great test of the Kickstarter system, which is designed to reward confidence, but punish overconfidence. What happened to requests by male and female entrepreneurs? Given that projects launched by a woman tended to have more reasonable goals, these projects were more likely to get funded than projects launched by a man. Score one for realistic thinking.

The researchers also found that men were more likely than women to be serial founders of projects. While the overall balance of men and women in the Kickstarter sample was fifty-six percent men and forty-four percent women, a very different picture emerged if you looked only at entrepreneurs who had launched at least five projects. More than seventy percent of these serial entrepreneurs were men, fewer than thirty percent were women. Men were also far more likely than women to launch a second project on Kickstarter after their first attempt failed to reach its fund-raising goal. Did they succeed the second or third time? No, the researchers found that one of the best predictors of fund-raising success was *prior* fund-raising success. Someone who asks for five hundred thousand dollars and fails is likely to fail the next time, when they ask for four hundred thousand dollars. Since individual women were less likely than individual men to fail the first time, individual women were more likely than individual men to succeed when they launched second or third efforts. Score two for realistic thinking.

When the researchers stepped back and looked at the big picture, however, something curious happened: As a group, men were more successful than women in getting projects funded via Kickstarter. How could this be? If men are delusionally overconfident and are punished for delusional overconfidence, how can many more men than women end up being successful? Well, there are multiple reasons for this—including sexism. But one important reason has to do with the power of self-deception. Men are *so* delusionally overconfident that they refuse to take failure as a useful signal. They keep launching new projects, and keep asking for large sums of money. Since initial failure on Kickstarter is an excellent predictor of subsequent failure, a large number of these men fail. But so many men keep throwing their hats in the ring, and keep asking for large sums of money, that *some of them end up succeeding*. Overall, the researchers concluded, this is one of the factors that leads to gender disparities in entrepreneurial success. If you had to gauge the odds of a single man or a single woman succeeding on Kickstarter, you would pick the woman. But if you had to gauge the odds of one *group* succeeding more, you would pick men. Delusional overconfidence is very bad for many men as individuals, but the researchers found that as a *group*, it helps men succeed.

To be clear, unrealistic positive illusions can also be very helpful to women. In one study, Shelley Taylor found that such illusions were particularly potent—and useful—among women who had breast cancer. Many of the patients she studied unrealistically believed they had control over their disease. Of seventy-two women Taylor looked at in one study, only two said they were doing worse than most other women with breast cancer. Many of the women were exceptionally optimistic in ways that were not supported by the facts. In some cases, women on the brink of death insisted that they had beaten the disease.

These self-deceptions were helpful in a number of ways. Taylor found that women with greater positive illusions *coped better* with their cancer—they were less prone to suffer from the psychological problems that accompany the onset of a life-threatening disease, such as depression, feelings of worthlessness, insomnia, substance abuse, and suicidal impulses. Subsequent studies have confirmed these findings in other groups. In one study of heightened self-deception among gay men with AIDS, some patients claimed that they had "developed an immunity" or that their immune system was "more capable of fighting the AIDS virus than other gay men." Such self-deceptions also improved their ability to cope with the disease. It eased their suffering in ways that were real.

Delusional self-confidence in the face of entrepreneurial failure can be a source of resilience. False beliefs about how you are going to do better than others when facing down a disease can be adaptive. But such beliefs are also helpful *in general*. A wide array of research shows that people who are delusionally optimistic tend to outlive people with more realistic attitudes.

Joseph Enriquez was not facing a life-threatening illness. But his feelings of isolation, coupled with the devastating loss of his mother, his father's illness, and his unrequited longing for a life partner, produced a desperation not unlike that of a cancer patient. He had two options: He could see reality clearly, and accept a life of rejection. Or he could create the illusion of romance from something that was not real, by ignoring the many warning sings that his relationship with Pamala was largely inside his own head. Was his choice any less adaptive than the illusions of patients with terminal illnesses, or the willingness of a pet owner to sacrifice his life savings to prolong the life of an aging cat? Just like the delusional entrepreneurs and the optimistic breast cancer patients, Joseph Enriquez had plenty of evidence—if he wanted to see it—that could have shown him Pamala was not real. He had never spoken to her or met her in person. She never made direct references to anything he had written. Her letters were invariably positive and affectionate, but they were vague—"I can see you are a good person" or "I can see that you need a friend." (Who isn't and who doesn't?) For the seduction to work, Joseph had to actively participate—he had to suspend disbelief in order to construct the fantasy. His self-deception clearly played a role in the success of Don Lowry's deception. It's understandable that, from the outside, from the perspective of our own naive realism, we might want to scream at Joseph to throw away the letters unread. We might want to tell him that this was a "fake relationship." But subjectively, the relationship felt more intense and meaningful to Joseph than the "real relationships" that populated his life.

Who gets to decide if Joseph made a terrible mistake? Who gets to decide that water labeled *L'eau du Robinet* is "bullshit," that an iPhone is not worth several hundred dollars more than a Samsung phone, or that spending thousands of dollars on a kidney transplant for a cat is a waste of money? When we call Joseph's relationship "fake," isn't this a little like atheists telling religious people that their relationship with God is "fake"? Joseph's response, like that of many religious people confronted by well-meaning atheists, might fairly be described like this: "Why do you get to decide what feels subjectively true for me?" He was not alone. Many members of Don Lowry's "Church of Love" found the concerns of journalists and prosecutors to be paternalistic. In response to concerns that the hoax had to be brought to an end, some said they had never belonged to another organization that provided better value for money.

6

Predictive Reasoning

> *Love is like a tree: it grows by itself, roots itself deeply in*
> *our being and continues to flourish over a heart in ruin. The*
> *inexplicable fact is that the blinder it is, the more tenacious it is.*
> *It is never stronger than when it is completely unreasonable.*

Victor Hugo, *The Hunchback of Notre-Dame*

We are easily deceived by those with whom we have formed emotional attachments. This is true of our relationships with our friends, our parents and our children, but it is particularly so when it comes to our romantic partners. Once Joseph fell in love, deceptions that would seem ridiculous to an outside observer became plausible to him. It's easy to conclude that Joseph fooled himself into believing something that wasn't real. It's harder to see, but is equally true, that delusional thinking and positive illusions shape most "healthy" relationships. An abundance of studies have explored the role of positive illusions in romantic love. Many of these studies have concluded that the more we deceive ourselves about our lovers—the more we believe our partners are kind and generous and beautiful, for example—the happier our relationships will be.

The philosopher Alain de Botton has written that we will all "marry the wrong person." It's a claim that often provokes a strong reaction. But de Botton is not making a case for divorce. Quite the opposite. He argues that, to make marriage work, we need to deal with the inevitable imperfections of our partners. De Botton wants us to reject the "founding Romantic idea upon which the Western understanding of marriage has been based the last two hundred and fifty years: that a perfect being exists who can meet all our needs and satisfy our every yearning." In reality, "every human will frustrate, anger, annoy, madden and disappoint us—and we will (without any malice) do the same to them."

How to solve this unsolvable problem? An array of psychological research studies show that in most healthy relationships, people see their partners through rose-tinted glasses: We see them as *better* people than objective analysis would justify. But we also see them as the *sort* of better people that we want to be with, based upon our own ideals and biases of what kind of person we imagine to be "just right."

One Canadian study of positive illusions asked married and dating couples to rate themselves and their partners on an array of personality characteristics that compose what psychologists call the "interpersonal circle," things like kindness, empathy and tolerance. They were also asked to rate a hypothetical "ideal partner." Not only did the subjects routinely judge their partners to be better all around compared to the way their partners evaluated themselves, their images of their partners was particularly inflated in the areas of personality that the subjects cared about the most. The more someone valued kindness, for example, the more they exaggerated how kind their partners were. Perhaps the most important part of the study was that the researchers found that the couples who had the most inflated views of their partners—the ones who saw their relationships with the greatest degree of self-deception—were the happiest. This is hardly a new idea: Benjamin Franklin once offered the advice, "Keep your eyes wide open before marriage—and half-shut afterward."

Imagine extending the kind of well-meaning advice we might give to Joseph Enriquez to all the couples we know. When ministers at weddings say, "Should anyone here present know of any reason that this couple should not be joined in holy matrimony, speak now or forever hold your peace," hands ought to shoot up. Doesn't rationality and truth-telling demand that we set these deluded couples straight? "No," we ought to clamor, "you're wrong. She is most definitely not the most beautiful woman in the world." Or, "Are you kidding? You think that guy is a dependable rock? He's a hot mess!"

An array of cognitive distortions also helps keep couples *faithful* to one another. People who are in love are quicker to denigrate potential alternatives to their current romantic partner. In one study, psychologists asked heterosexual subjects to write a short essay about a time when they felt love toward their partner, while a control group was asked to write instead about happiness. The subjects were then placed before a computer screen and shown pictures of attractive members of the opposite sex, along with shapes like squares and circles, which they were asked to identify as quickly as possible. The people who had been asked to think about their love interests were better able to block out the images of attractive alternatives—they were "repulsed," in the words of the researchers—and identify the geometric shapes more quickly.

Other studies show that people who are in love underrate the virtues of alternate partners—seeing them as less attractive and less available—in the same manner that they overrate their current partners. Those in the strongest relationships tend to underrate potential temptations the most. "Even if the grass is greener on the other side of the fence," the authors of one study wrote, "happy gardeners would be less likely to notice."

More recently, neurologists have actually unveiled brain processes that cause some of these self-deceptions. When we are in love, brain changes literally impair our critical thinking ability (which is why it can be difficult to argue a sixteen-year-old out of a crush). Interestingly, the same changes can be triggered by maternal love, which can be even more unreasonable. The positive illusions about the personalities and traits of those we love the most lead us to be, in a very literal sense, blind to their flaws. Psychologists call this the "love-is-blind bias."

Love is hardly the only emotion that causes our perceptions to be led astray. A great many emotions cause us to see what we want to see. Most people look in a mirror about thirty times a day. If many of us see our romantic partners as more attractive than they really are, it turns out we also see *ourselves* as better looking than we really are. In one experiment (which led to a research paper titled "Mirror, Mirror on the Wall"), subjects were presented with a series of photographs of themselves that were altered to fit predetermined archetypes of beautiful and ugly people. Subjects were asked to pick their unmodified picture from a series of eleven altered photographs. Rather immodestly, most people chose pictures that made them look more attractive. People with higher self-esteem seemed to overrate their own looks more than people with low self-esteem, another piece of evidence that superior psychological functioning is often linked to delusional thinking.

At Montclair State University, researchers have analyzed a part of the brain that appears to be vitally important for the production of self-deception. This brain region seems to be involved in triggering positive illusions and high self-regard. The researchers examined what happens when you temporarily *disable* this part of the brain—the medial prefrontal cortex. In one study, a dozen participants were brought into a lab and fitted with Lycra swim caps and protective earplugs. The volunteers agreed to be subjected to transcranial magnetic stimulation, in order to produce a temporary lesion in their medial prefrontal cortex. When the magnetic stimulation was off, and the self-deceiving medial prefrontal cortex was active, volunteers chose positive adjectives to describe themselves. But when the magnetic stimulation was on—and the medial prefrontal cortex was partially disabled—volunteers preferred more modest adjectives to describe themselves. Unsurprisingly, volunteers subjected to such brain modulation felt more depressed—and disliked the intervention.

Psychiatrist Iain McGilchrist thinks the propensity of the brain to deceive itself is at least partly connected to the hemispheric division in the brain. The right hemisphere, according to McGilchrist, is more self-aware of its limitations, whereas the left hemisphere is prone to blithe self-deception. Patients with strokes to their left hemisphere, for example, have a functioning right hemisphere and usually know they have had a stroke, but patients with right-hemisphere strokes delusionally think they are OK. McGilchrist thinks self-deception is largely driven by the left hemisphere's unrealistic desire to see itself as being in control. In an interview for *Hidden Brain*, McGilchrist told me about an exchange at a hospital bed that he also describes in his book, *The Master and His Emissary*. A doctor is interrogating a patient who has suffered a right hemisphere stroke—she only has use of the self-deceiving left hemisphere. The doctor asks the patient about her left arm. Since the patient has had a right hemisphere stroke, this arm is paralyzed. How does the patient explain the inoperable arm attached to her body?

EXAMINER: Whose arm is this?

AR (PATIENT): It's not mine.

EXAMINER: Whose is it?

AR: It's my mother's.

EXAMINER: How on earth does it happen to be here?

AR: I don't know. I found it in my bed.

We not only see what we want to see in a figurative sense, we also see what we want to see quite literally. One of the earliest experiments to identify our capacity for what psychologists call "wishful seeing" was conducted in 1947 by Harvard professor Jerome Bruner. He was born blind, and spent much of his life trying to understand the relationship between what our eyes see in the world around us, and what our minds *perceive*. Bruner argued that our own minds—with all their hopes and desires and prejudices—play a powerful role in our perception of reality.

Bruner's experiment was conducted among two groups of children, one drawn from wealthy backgrounds and another from poor families. The children were all given various coins, ranging from a penny to a fifty-cent piece. They were then asked to estimate how big the coins were. All the children perceived the coins to be bigger than they actually were. Their visual perception was influenced by desire. But the poor children perceived the coins to be even bigger than the rich children because, Bruner theorized, their desire for money—their need for it—was greater.

Today, some of the most important work on our tendency to see what we want to see has been done by a pair of social psychologists, New York University's Emily Balcetis and Michigan State University's David Dunning. (Dunning is probably even better known for his research paper "Unskilled and Unaware of It," which explores what is now called the Dunning-Kruger Effect, the tendency for people who are *really* bad at something to think they are good at it.)

Balcetis and Dunning actually coined the term "wishful seeing" as they were conducting a 2006 study on the influence of desire on visual perception. One of the experiments in the study involved a group of volunteers who took part in what had been advertised as a "taste testing experiment." The subjects were told that a symbol was going to flash on their computer screens. Depending on whether the symbol was a number or a letter, they would be served either a delicious glass of freshly squeezed orange juice or what was described as a "gelatinous, chunky, green, foul-smelling, somewhat viscous concoction labeled as an organic veggie smoothie."

In fact, the same image appeared before each of the subjects: an ambiguous figure that could be read as either the number "13" or the letter "B." If the subject had been told the orange juice would be served with a number, they were much more likely to see a "13." If they were told that it would be served with a letter, they tended to see a "B."

Balcetis and Dunning have also found that objects can appear to be closer depending on how much we desire them. In one experiment, half the subjects ate salty pretzels, while the rest were given water to drink. They were then all asked to estimate their distance from a water bottle that was a few feet away from where they were sitting. Those who had eaten the pretzels—and were thirsty—saw the water as being closer than the control group. Fear can produce similar distortions: People asked to judge the proximity of a tarantula saw it as closer if they were afraid of spiders. Those who were the most afraid saw the tarantula as closest of all.

In every one of these cases, reality is being distorted by hidden systems in the brain. But what is most interesting is that reality is being distorted *in systematic ways* to cause us to reach particular conclusions. In other words, these are not merely errors, they are *biases* designed to lead us to predetermined goals. When such biases are shared by large numbers of people, they can produce events that change the course of history.

In October 1917, a huge crowd gathered near the Portuguese town of Fátima. They were drawn there by an account of three local shepherd children, two of whom would go on to be canonized. That spring, the children, the oldest of whom was ten, experienced a series of miraculous visitations, first from an angel, and then from the Virgin Mary herself, who was said to reveal three prophecies. The Virgin Mary also told them that on October thirteenth, she would return to the spot where they stood and perform a great miracle for all to see. The story of the Children of Fátima quickly gained traction among the devout in Catholic Portugal. Despite the fact that two days of rain turned roads to mud and made travel difficult that October, as many as one hundred thousand people turned out on the day the miracle was scheduled to occur.

At first, the crowd was treated only to more rain. Then around midday, the weather broke, and many of the people began shouting and pointing at the sky. Seventeen-year-old Dominic Reis, who had traveled a hundred miles to be there, later gave this account: "Around noon time, the sun started breaking through the clouds and we could see the sun. Now it was raining just like you open a faucet in your house. Rain! And then suddenly the rain stopped. The sun started to roll from one place to another, changing blue, yellow, all colors. Then we see the sun come toward the children, toward the tree. Everyone was hollering out. We were all so afraid. Some started to confess their sins openly before everyone. Even my mother grabbed me to herself and started to cry, saying 'Dominic, this is the end of the world.'"

The event is usually recalled as the Miracle of the Sun. What exactly the miracle was, however, is not clear. Everyone in the crowd that day seemed to see something different. One man present described the sun as a revolving ball of snow. Others said "the sun whirled on itself like a giant Catherine wheel and that it lowered itself to the earth as if to burn it in its rays." One woman recalled that the sun "turned into a sheet of silver which broke up as the clouds were torn apart and the silver sun, enveloped in the same gauzy grey light, was seen to whirl and turn." Another said that "the sun appeared to stop spinning . . . and to dance in the sky until it seemed to detach itself from its place and fall upon us." Others, including the three Children of Fátima themselves, claimed to see the face of the Virgin Mary gazing at them from the sky. But many people saw nothing unusual at all. And despite the fact that there were many photographers present, none managed to take a picture that captured anything out of the ordinary.

It is possible that the Miracle of the Sun was an astronomical event, perhaps what is known as a sundog, an optical illusion caused by the refraction of light off ice, creating the illusion of multiple suns. But that wouldn't explain the vast divergence in the accounts of what so many people saw. A more likely explanation is that the crowd was simply swayed by the power of suggestion, expectation and hope. Most of the people who had gathered that day, like young Dominic Reis and his family, had trekked vast distances on a pilgrimage. They wanted to be present for a promised event. They came expecting to see a miracle, and so they saw one.

If there is an American equivalent of the Miracle of the Sun, it might be the craze for spirit photography that engulfed the nation in the middle of the nineteenth century, shortly after the widespread introduction of photography itself. The first spirit photograph was produced by a jewelry engraver from Boston named William Mumler, who dabbled in photography in his spare time and hit upon a method to produce intentional double exposures, which allowed him to superimpose faint, ghostlike images over existing photographs. His first known spirit photo was of himself with his recently deceased cousin hovering ghost-like in the background.

Word spread around Boston, and he was soon asked to produce a spirit photograph of Luther Colby, the editor of the spiritualist newspaper, *The Banner of Light*. The photograph Mumler produced showed the image of a Native American chief named "Wapanaw" standing by the newspaperman's side. *The Banner of Light* was the most read spiritualist publication in the United States, and its advocacy caused a surge of interest in Mumler's work. The jewelry engraver embraced his new role as a broker of what he called "spirit-communion" and claimed to have gained knowledge of a "future existence, and in the invisible host that surrounds us."

Despite a great deal of skepticism and outright ridicule—the famous showman and skeptic P. T. Barnum was one of his fiercest critics—Mumler's business took off. It wasn't uncommon for people to leave his studio in tears, overwhelmed at having seen the spirit of a deceased child or spouse. His clients included some of New York and Boston's most well-to-do families. His most famous photograph was of Mary Todd Lincoln, with the ghostly visage of her late husband, President Abraham Lincoln, hovering over her shoulder.

Mumler was eventually charged with fraud after some of the "spirits" in his photos were shown to be very much alive. He was tried in New York City. P. T. Barnum was one of those who testified against him. (The showman mirthfully hired a photographer to doctor an image of himself with Abraham Lincoln's spirit in the background.) But Mumler was able to draw on a parade of former clients to testify on his behalf, people who were convinced that his photographs contained priceless images of their deceased loved ones. Although the publicity surrounding the trial crippled his business, Mumler was acquitted.

A century and a half later, it is easy to write off the people who fell for William Mumler's photographs as the kind of people who would believe anything. In truth, those who embraced the American spiritualist movement tended to be better educated and better off than the average American. Spiritualism was in many ways an attempt to meld religion and science, to use the latest technologies to better understand the spiritual world. Spirit photography was a way to "prove" the existence of another realm.

It is revealing that spirit photography emerged when it did. American photography in its early years had a strong association with death. Its advent coincided with the Civil War, the bloodiest conflict in the history of the United States. For the first time, newspapers ran pictures of battlefields, bringing the carnage into the homes of ordinary people. Soldiers often had their photos taken before departing for war, and these images became every parent's cherished memorial to lost sons. Spirit photography was a way to soothe the grieving, to satisfy what the writer Ann Braude has called the "hunger for communion with the dead." The pictures may look creepy or crude today, but they were once a source of comfort, proof that loved ones were not *truly* gone. Not surprisingly, spirit photography experienced a revival in Europe after the First World War, when one of its most famous champions was the physician and Sherlock Holmes-creator Arthur Conan Doyle.

There are, of course, an endless supply of examples like the Miracle of the Sun or the photographs of William Mumler, where people see things that do not exist simply because they are desperate to see them. Not all these illusions involve the supernatural: Sports fans will tirelessly review controversial plays in slow motion, and see completely different things depending on their team loyalties. Most of us are never going to see the Virgin Mary in a piece of toast, or anywhere else for that matter. But we all share something in common with the people who do: Our hopes, needs and desires shape what we see in the world.

Our senses are flooded with information. We literally do not have the cognitive power to process all of this data, and so our brains take a shortcut. They discard most of the information, and focus attention on a small subset of the data. This is one reason we fall for illusions in psychological experiments. When you ask people to keep very close track of basketballs being passed back and forth by a group of players on a court, about half fail to notice an actor in a gorilla suit who walks into the frame, beats his chest, and walks out. (There are popular videos on YouTube that demonstrate this experiment.)

We think we are taking in everything that we see, but really, even when we are watching something as specific as a basketball game, we are primarily paying attention to *a small number of things*. Our expectations tell us what to attend to, and what to ignore. When we witness a familiar scene—a group of people playing basketball—the mental picture in our heads is influenced by the many previous games of basketball we have seen. We simply don't expect to see a chest-beating gorilla on a basketball court—which is why we don't notice it when it shows up. (Of course, if you now go online and track down a video of the gorilla-basketball experiment, you probably *will* see the gorilla, because now you are expecting it.) A fire hydrant is much easier to identify when it is on a street corner. But put it in the middle of a living room? It takes longer to spot, if you spot it at all.

In recent years, scientists have shown that the conventional model of how we think our brains work is spectacularly wrong. We imagine that our eyes behave like a camera, taking in the world and producing a pictorial representation in our heads. But this isn't what actually happens—and if you gave it some thought, you would understand why this *cannot* be what happens. When you look out at the world, the first thing your brain does is orient itself. It asks, "Do I know the thing I am seeing? Have I seen it before? Do I know what to expect?" In other words, your brain looks for a familiar *model* of what it is seeing based on past experience.

Why do it this way, instead of simply taking in the world as it appears? Because taking in the entire world on a moment-to-moment basis would be impossibly costly in terms of brain processing. And much of the time, our brains need to be doing many things at once. You are driving a car, but your attention is also focused on the conversation you are having with a friend in the passenger seat. Rather than devote scarce mental resources to analyzing all the gigabits of information that are surging into your brain from your senses, it's more efficient (if less accurate) to fall back on models that already exist about what you are taking in. As you drive, your brain constantly generates these models—you pull up at a traffic light waiting to make a left turn, and your brain draws on its vast repository of experience of what happens at traffic lights during left turns.

"But wait," you say, "it's not as if when I look at a tree, I can only see one tree—my mental model of a tree. No, I can see an infinite variety of trees—dead ones, living ones, birches, maples and coconut trees." That's true, and that gets to what your brain is actually doing with the information flowing in from your eyes. Rather than take in the *entire tree*, and have to do all the mental processing of huge amounts of data to determine that it is in fact a tree, your brain generates a model of a tree and then modifies it *a little bit* based on the input coming in from your eyes. This way, you only need the limited data required to paint in the details of this particular tree. The basic tree—its *treeness*, if you will—is generated automatically, instantly and unconsciously based on the tens of thousands of trees you've seen before.

There is another trick our brains play on us: Even as they process very little of the information entering our eyes and other senses, even as they substitute models and preexisting knowledge for what we are actually seeing, they give us the *illusion* that we are taking in everything around us. Tell someone they are not really seeing a tree, but seeing their *mental model* of a tree, and they will bristle. But this, too, makes perfect sense from an evolutionary perspective: Why bother making you feel like you have an inadequate and fragile grasp of reality? It might be the truth, but how does that improve your evolutionary fitness? Why would generating such insecurity help you function more effectively, or lead you to find a mate?

Since most of us are experts at doing these sorts of mental gymnastics, it can be difficult to intuitively experience how our brains are constantly generating models of the world. One way to observe this phenomenon in action, however, is to think about language. Fluent speakers can pick up what someone is saying in a noisy bar. They are able to do this because they are very skilled at filling in all the things their ears do not actually hear. As you lean in to listen to a friend, your brain does exactly the same thing it did with the trees or at the traffic intersection. It builds a model of the conversation and, before your friend says something, you are already half-expecting what she will say. You then use your ears to fill in what's missing. (This is why machines designed to pick up sounds far fainter than the human ear can detect are often inferior to humans when it comes to understanding language. The machines are trying to process language the hard way—the way you *think* your brain is doing it. The machines are taking in gobs of data, trying to pick out the words, trying to construct meaning out of sentences. Your brain, on the other hand, is using its vast repositories of knowledge and experience to *predict* where the conversation is going, and only using audio information to fill in the gaps.) It's the same with written language. Yu cn understnd this sentence, wth all its splllng mstkes, becoz yr brain is exptrtly fillng in whats missng.

But this tendency we have to quickly construct mental models can also be our downfall: Experts can be worse than novices at seeing things that are out of the ordinary, because experience has made them very skilled at generating models. They are less reliant than beginners on what their eyes are actually telling them. I once spent twenty minutes on the internet staring at this puzzle:

CAN **YOU** FIND THE
THE **MISTAKE?**

1   2   3   4   5   6   7   8   9

Eventually, I gave up. When I looked up the answer, I found it incomprehensible that I had failed to see the mistake. One way to spot the mistake for yourself is to read like a beginner: Put your finger on each word and read it aloud, stop for a second and then move to the next word. If you did that and now realize what you missed, congratulations. The reason you missed it when you read it the first time was because your brain expertly generated a model of the sentence. This model matched the syntax of thousands of sentences you'd read before. You didn't see the extra word because that word was like the chest-beating gorilla who appears in the middle of a basketball game, or the fire hydrant that shows up in your living room.

All of this suggests the brain has robust machinery to subvert and supplant what our eyes and ears are actually reporting, as well as the dictates of logic and reason. The brain comes preloaded with directives—*Protect your kids! Run to safety! Fall in love!*—and rapidly learns in the early years of childhood to form models of the world. The goal is not to waste precious mental resources on the unimportant task of seeing reality accurately, but instead to focus on the far more important tasks of survival and reproduction— what evolutionary biologists call *fitness*.

Long before psychologists and neuroscientists began investigating the brain systematically, at least two groups of laypeople realized they had a lot to gain by studying the mind: magicians and con artists. Magicians understood that even when people think they are paying close attention to something, the limitations of the brain prevent them from taking in most of what is really going on. They discovered that the brain is a story-generation machine, and therefore vulnerable to narratives—and red herrings. They realized that our expectations powerfully shape what we see, and that by manipulating those expectations, they could control how we think and what we see.

Like magicians, con artists and charlatans have long understood that the human capacity for understanding and rationality is "bounded," that our capacity for logic and reason is hemmed in by our hopes and fears. For thousands of years, swindlers and hucksters have been using the machinery of the self-deceiving brain to turn us into marks.

Many aspects of the scam that came to be known as the Church of Love capitalized on its founder's intuitive grasp of psychology. Don Lowry had an uncanny understanding of—and knack for exploiting—human nature. He picked up some of his knowledge from years spent working as a copywriter for small ad agencies, and some from his father, a professor who taught psychology at Penn State. When he first conceived of writing love letters to men in the voices of dozens of fictitious women, he understood that the loneliness of his marks would drive their belief in the illusory world he was creating. (This insight is often employed by scammers. The most sophisticated cons don't trick victims as much as they set up the right conditions for victims to trick themselves.) In many letters, for example, the women Lowry invented claimed to be fleeing from something—an abusive family, poverty or drug addiction. The initial letters were often not flirtatious, but pleas for help and guidance. Lowry discovered his most loyal customers weren't sex perverts, but nice men who desperately wanted to feel needed. Many members were eager to embrace the role of benefactor and protector, and reveled in the notion that they could be knights in shining armor.

When the women said that they lived in a cloistered retreat, it conjured religious metaphors that have brought people to houses of worship for thousands of years. The women were called "Angels," and the retreat bore striking resemblance to a nunnery. The Angels claimed to lead a spartan existence, sleeping in a communal, barracks-like annex, and passing their days tending to their vegetable plots and sewing their own clothes. Most of them had sworn off alcohol and drugs, and had to live under strict rules of chastity. Lowry's central character, Mother Maria, was a quasi-mystical figure. If the young women writing love letters promised *romantic* love, Mother Maria promised *motherly* love, tinged with salvation. She was occasionally referred to as an Archangel, and was said to possess supernatural powers, including the ability to brew potions that could extend the human life span. She supposedly had a psychic ability called "Telesthesia" that gave her the power to exert a positive influence over the lives of members through special rituals.

The masterstroke in the fantasy was an idyllic Garden-of-Eden-like paradise that the Angels claimed to be building: Chonda-Za, a thinly disguised play on Shangri-La, from James Hilton's novel *Lost Horizon*. It was to be a utopian world, an idyllic community where members of the Church of Love could one day live out their days with the Angels. Of course, building this utopia meant acquiring land, constructing living quarters, and other organizational fees and overhead. Anyone who wanted to live in such a place needed to be a member in good standing with the Church of Love—in other words, someone who was generous with his Love Offerings. The biggest benefactors were given various Masonic-sounding titles, the highest of which was "Temple Master."

With this strange, anachronistic combination of Tinder and a quasi-religious commune, Lowry managed to convince thousands of men that they were in deeply meaningful, even spiritual, relationships with Angels. Some men signed "Mystic Marriage Pledges" that bound them to their chosen Angel when the paradise of Chonda-Za was eventually completed. (Since the letters were sent out in bulk, Angel Vanessa was "married" to many men, each of whom thought he was in an exclusive relationship with her.) At its peak in the early 1980s, the Church of Love had more than thirty thousand members throughout the United States and Canada, and revenues in excess of a million dollars a year. Over the years, members also sent the Angels vast numbers of gifts—televisions, candies, clothes and lingerie. Lowry opened a second-hand store called Savers Haven to resell the items to the good citizens of Moline.

7

Somewhere Over the Rainbow

All are lunatics, but he who can analyze his delusion is called a philosopher.

Ambrose Bierce

In the early 1950s, a Chicago housewife named Dorothy Martin—a dabbler in automatic writing and Scientology, and, like Don Lowry, a fan of the novel *Lost Horizon*—began receiving messages beamed into her head from a distant planet called "Clarion." The messages warned that a "supreme being" was going to cause a series of devastating natural disasters that would destroy the earth. Only those who joined her movement would be saved, spirited away to safety by a UFO that was to arrive at her home four days before the great cataclysm was to begin: an enormous flood that would submerge the city of Chicago on December 21, 1955.

Martin's prophecy attracted a determined band of followers, many of whom quit their jobs and gave up their homes to prepare for the end times. Some were drawn by newspaper advertisements that proclaimed the end of the world. The advertisements also caught the eye of a young University of Minnesota psychologist named Leon Festinger, who infiltrated the group in hopes of studying the after-effects of a prophecy that failed to materialize. He fully expected Martin's followers to lose their faith. But when December 21 came and went without floods or UFOs, the most committed of Martin's followers grew *stronger* in their commitment. They doubled down.

Festinger documented his experiences in his book *When Prophecies Fail*. His great contribution was the concept of cognitive dissonance: It is painful to hold opposing ideas in our minds, and we seek ways to relieve this conflict. Martin's followers deeply believed in the prophecy. If they were to admit they were wrong, they would also have to acknowledge that giving up their homes and quitting their jobs was foolish. They would have to admit their devotion to the cause was irrational and misguided. At the same time, the facts were telling them that they *had* made a mistake. As Festinger discovered, holding opposing notions is painful, and people look for ways to remove this source of pain. If sacrificing the facts can ease the unpleasant feeling, the facts turn out to be expendable.

Cognitive dissonance helps explain a lot about the world— from voters who refuse to acknowledge they made a mistake in electing a demagogue to organizations that fail to back away from misguided policies, even in the face of mounting evidence. It also helps explain why members of the Church of Love continued to cling to their beliefs, even as details of the scam were revealed. As I learned the details of Joseph Enriquez's final months as a member of the Church of Love—and the way he looks back on those years—I found it hard not to think about Dorothy Martin and Leon Festinger.

. . .

In 1986, Joseph received a letter that was different than the ones he had previously recieved. In it, Pamala suggested something new: She asked to meet. After years of longing, long-distance fantasies and imaginings, the idea of meeting Pamala was thrilling. She told him the meeting would be in Moline, Illinois, and was to celebrate her birthday. Joseph made arrangements for the trip. When he arrived, he was overjoyed to see her: Pamala was just as beautiful as she was in her photos. But Joseph was also disconcerted: There were about a dozen other men at the gathering. And it appeared these other men were also in love with Pamala.

It felt like a kick in the stomach. Joseph didn't quite understand what was happening. But he refused to let the other men deter him. He knew how he felt about Pamala, and how she felt about him. He knew she liked music boxes, so he had bought her one as a present. When she opened his gift in front of the other men, and the music box played "When The Saints Go Marching In," he felt like they really did have a special relationship. Pamala clearly loved the present. Joseph was ecstatic. As the music played, he experienced an unfamiliar feeling: He felt the eyes of the other men on him, and he realized that they were jealous. It made him happy.

Joseph's situation was more complicated than that of many other members of Don Lowry's love letter scheme. In writing Pamala's love letters, Lowry had used the name of a woman who had at one point been the Church of Love's marketing director. The photos of Pamala St. Charles that adorned Joseph's house were of a woman who was actually named Pamala St. Charles—and it was the same woman who organized and was present at the meeting in Moline.*

---

* After Pamala St. Charles was released from prison, she moved away and changed her name. She declined to be interviewed about her experience with the Church of Love. Elsewhere, including on social media, she has said that she was misled by Donald Lowry, and was a victim of his abuse.

This Pamala St. Charles wasn't *really* the woman in the letters Joseph had received for so long—those were written by Don Lowry. When Joseph first met Pamala, however, he could be forgiven for mistaking the two. In our interview, I asked him whether he asked Pamala at the meeting whether she had written him the letters. Joseph said he had not. From his point of view, this was understandable. How many of us question things that are deeply woven into the fabric of our lives?

Joseph's story has something in common with the plot of the movie *The Truman Show*. Jim Carrey plays a character trapped in a reality TV program. Truman's entire life is a fiction. His wife, his best friends, the people he passes on the street—all of them are actors. Millions of people around the world tune in to see what Truman will do next. He is the only one who doesn't know what is actually going on.

When I first spoke to Joseph, I wanted to understand how he felt when he discovered the relationship with Pamala was not what he thought it was. I pressed him over and over to talk about that moment when they first met, when he discovered, as he put it, that things were not as they had seemed. To me, looking in from the outside, it seemed obvious that Joseph would see through the deception, that he would be outraged to discover he was the victim of a con. He would investigate and find out that it was not Pamala who had written all those love letters to him. His questions would eventually lead him to Don Lowry, the mastermind behind the Church of Love, and the author of the letters.

What I failed to realize, during that initial interview, was that Joseph was a lot like Jim Carrey's character in *The Truman Show*. By the time he met Pamala for the first time, Joseph was so deeply in love with her that questioning the veracity of their relationship meant calling into question some of the most important things in his life. Pamala was his lodestar, his soulmate. When he discovered she had other paramours, he was stunned and sad, but it didn't erase his feelings for her. Joseph didn't see the other men who showed up to celebrate Pamala's birthday as a betrayal; he saw it as a *setback*. And he knew what he had to do when confronted by setbacks—Pamala herself had told him. On numerous occasions when he felt his life was falling apart, Pamala's letters had lifted him up from the depths. "Get back on your feet," she had once written, and he felt that she had seen right into his soul. How could he question the integrity of the person who had saved his life? It was unthinkable.

In *The Truman Show*, one major impediment to Truman discovering the truth is that his deceivers were clever. But there was an even bigger hurdle: Piercing the deception required Truman to jettison everything that he held dear. He had to give up attachments and friendships. He had to recognize that his friends were not his friends, that his job was not his job, that his wife was not his wife. It was exactly the same with Joseph. Pamala had brought things into his life that he didn't have, things he thought he would never have—things he had now come to believe he could not live *without*: She had brought him love and companionship and trust. She had brought him comfort and happiness and hope. He was a lonely man in a remote town in dusty Texas. He had few prospects. She was his oasis. She was his friend. He had hoped she would be his wife. To question whether the Pamala who stood before him at the meeting in Moline was the same Pamala who had written him letters would have meant discarding the armor that protected him, the anchor that stabilized him, the beacon that guided him.

In the weeks and months that followed that initial meeting, the same dynamic would play out again and again. Joseph would be asked, in effect, whether he was willing to accept that the things that held his life together were a lie. And over and over, Joseph would answer that question in the negative.

Shortly after the birthday party in Moline, Joseph began to hear that Pamala was in trouble. Investigators were circling, and Joseph learned that Pamala was going to be charged with a crime. He learned about Don Lowry and the letter-writing scheme, but Joseph told himself that the Pamala he'd met was the same woman he had loved. When he was asked to testify at a trial in Peoria where Don Lowry and Pamala St. Charles were being charged with various counts of mail fraud and conspiracy, Joseph agreed to testify—for the defense.

Some of the men Joseph had met at Pamala's birthday also showed up at the trial. Suddenly, they were no longer competitors for Pamala's affections. They were part of the same tribe: They were the deluded members of an organization that the media treated derisively. The public mocked them. Reporters hurled questions at them. Onlookers laughed at them.

To the bewilderment of prosecutors and the media, the men whom Joseph had befriended stood outside the courtroom holding placards in support of the defendants. They criticized government prosecutors who were ostensibly trying to protect them from a con man. One cold winter day, as (the real) Pamala St. Charles was entering court, Joseph saw that journalists were hounding her. He rushed over and protectively draped his own coat around her shoulders. He escorted her into the courtroom "like a bodyguard."

In time, I came to see that men like Carl Cornell (the guest on *Geraldo* described in the Introduction) and Joseph Enriquez were being courageous. In the face of vitriolic criticism and hyperbolic ridicule, they stood their ground, and defended the women they believed they loved. If the world had a problem with that, they said, the world be damned.

. . .

When I interviewed Joseph, we spent a lot of time talking about the trial in Peoria. Surely, I thought, it would be at this point that the scales would fall from his eyes. But the trial did little to change Joseph's views. The entire trial—held, ironically, in a former post office—played out like a case study of cognitive dissonance. Investigators laid out a clear and damning portrait of Don Lowry's scheme. Right from the opening statement, Prosecutor Tate Chambers made clear that the scheme operated like a fairy tale or a bedtime story:

> *When Maria Mireles was a young child in Mexico she had a religious experience. A spirit appeared to her and told her to go to the United States and to create a new Garden of Eden, a place called Chonda-Za, where men and women could live in harmony with nature once again.*

Chambers eventually made his way to a theatrical climax when he told the jury there "were no cold, hungry young women living on a Retreat in Hillsdale, Illinois. The money and the gifts that members sent did not go to fix the car, to repair the motor on the well, to buy food and clothes for the Angels." Pointing at Don Lowry, Chambers said, "It went to him."

As befitted everything about his scheme, Don Lowry's defense was unorthodox. In the press, it would come to be called the "Santa Claus" defense. Defense Attorney Jerry Schick's opening statement included this memorable argument:

> *It is ironic here at the beginning of the Christmas season you are going to hear evidence that Don and his organization has created a fantasy, a fantasy like the fantasy that all of our children enjoy,*

*the fantasy of Santa Claus . . . The evidence in this case is evidence
of a fantasy. It is not evidence of fraud. This is a fantasy created by
Don Lowry for his members. Just as no harm comes to our children
from enjoying the fantasy of Santa Claus . . . no harm came to the
members by enjoying the fantasy of the Angels, Mother Maria,
the Retreat.*

Neither the prosecution nor the defense acknowledged the
complex psychological issues raised by the case. The prosecution's
contention was that Lowry had deliberately misled members into
believing something that wasn't true, and then profited from this
false belief. The defense wanted to show that Lowry was just a writer
and storyteller, and that his relationship with members was no different than the relationship between any novelist and his readers.

Certainly, the prosecution's version was closer to the truth. But
the very presence of men at the trial holding placards and cheer-
ing for the defendants suggested something deeper at work. If
there was deception—and there was—it involved complicity on
the part of members. Some testified they had made their way to
Hillsdale—the city in Illinois where all the letters from the Angels
were postmarked and where all the members sent in their "Love
Offerings"—in search of the Angels and the Retreat. Even among
those who testified for the prosecution, only a few voiced outrage
toward Don Lowry. Two members said the Church of Love had
saved them from suicide. One was a witness for the defense. The
other was a witness for the prosecution.

The defense witness, an unemployed thirty-five-year-old from
Massachusetts, described a life that, prior to joining the Church
of Love, "wasn't very meaningful or productive . . . just an empty
life with nothing, you know, nothing to strive for, nothing to look
forward to, no goals to speak of. I was just empty, lost and con-

fused." He said he had no friends, had abused alcohol and drugs, contemplated suicide. After connecting with the Angels, all that had "stopped immediately. Because I felt at that point I found something which, you know, gave my life some kind of direction, and meaning and purpose. And I just felt that I had found what I was looking for in life."

A prosecution witness, a custodian from Milwaukee, testified that he had fallen for Vanessa Covington, "a poor girl" whose "mother died in an accident by falling down some stairs." He had sent her a thousand dollars after she complained that "there was no food in the Retreat, and the girls were running around naked," and another eight hundred when the Angels needed a new sewing machine. He also sent Vanessa a new space heater so she could stay warm in the winter. In his will, he left everything "in the care of Vanessa and the Angels." A farmer from Indiana testified for the prosecution that he had sent "very sentimental" personal photos to the women at the Retreat. He believed the Angels were "going to be part of my family. I was going to be a family member."

Though several defense witnesses were coached to say that they understood the Church of Love was just a fantasy, many ended up revealing how deeply they had believed the fantasy. George Kulpaca first said his participation was merely "an outlet to correspond and keep myself busy . . . And I did enjoy that." But, under cross-examination, he admitted he believed the Angels were truly writing the letters themselves. The longest-tenured member to appear at trial was William Mills from St. Augustine, Florida, who had joined in 1979. He was called by the defense. Participating left him "feeling that I was part of this beautiful thing and this dream. It made me very happy." During the cross-examination, he said that he believed the money he sent to his beloved Angel Susan had paid for her hospital bills. "As far as I knew," he said, "that was what it was for."

Some members who testified at the trial were highly educated. One was a sitting professor of philosophy at Illinois State University. Another was a computer programmer who once sent in a Love Offering of six thousand dollars. There was an arbitrator from San Francisco. George Knox was a chemical engineer and a former executive at Dow Chemical. Prosecution witness Jerry Anderson was an aerospace engineer for Martin Marietta in Orlando where, according to his family, he worked on the space shuttle and the Hubbell Space Telescope. He was picked to testify precisely because of his accomplishments and to show, as Prosecutor Tate Chambers put it, that "anybody from a custodian to a rocket scientist could believe this. It isn't just uneducated people that believed in this. You can have a NASA engineer."

Anderson testified that he knew from the first letter that it had been produced with an "offset printing press." Yet he "believed that there was a young woman . . . who personally wrote each one of the letters." He had no doubt the Angels would one day build the dream community, Chonda-Za. "I believed it would be like a utopian community," he said. It would be a place where he could go, where "everyone could be happy." Starting in 1980, Anderson sent in thousands of dollars, once mailing a thousand-dollar check to one Angel as "a gift." George Seeger, a widowed industrial designer from Skokie, Illinois, sent a total of thirty-two thousand dollars. He truly believed in the Angels. He cared about the women. Much of the money he sent in was earmarked for the Angels to be able to take vacations. He saved his correspondence in a binder, with all the letters highlighted and heavily notated. His greatest worry was that his health problems would mean that he would never get to see the utopia of Chonda-Za. Some members imagined Chonda-Za as a kind of retirement community where they would spend their old age.

Others saw it as a pleasant and harmless fantasy. But lots of members embraced the mystical aspects of the story wholeheartedly.

Some of the most remarkable testimony about the supernatural appeal of Chonda-Za and the Church of Love came from a man named Ken Blanchard, a welder who testified for the prosecution. Decades later, I interviewed Blanchard near the small town where he lived in Iowa. I had a certain idea of the kind of person who would believe in Chonda-Za. Blanchard turned out to be nothing like I imagined. He came across as stolid and taciturn. He described himself as conservative—in a political sense, but also in every other sense. He wasn't the kind of man to try new things, or venture outside his comfort zone. Decades after his involvement with the Church of Love, Blanchard was still struggling to understand how he fell under Lowry's spell or had signed a "mystic marriage" pledge with "Angel Vanessa."

Blanchard said he was aware of the supernatural elements of the Church of Love from the outset. One of the first letters he received laid out Mother Maria's mystical abilities. "She was supposed to be able to lay her hands on a person who is ill and cure them." As time passed, letters touted Mother Maria's greatest power, a psychic ability to project her will across vast distances. Letters offered Blanchard the chance to take part in the "Circle of Love" or the "Angelic Telesthesia Ritual." Blanchard understood that Mother Maria would "have the Angels form a circle about her, and for one hour she and the Angels were to concentrate all their thoughts on me. And at the same time in my home I was to find a quiet spot and concentrate all of my thoughts on Maria and the Angels at the Retreat."

When he sent in a Love Offering to have the ritual performed, Mother Maria set a date. "On Saturday night at ten PM our time, I am going to focus all of my thoughts and energy on you," she wrote. "I am going to send to you warm and powerful vibrations across the miles to Griswold. It has come to me that you will be most receptive to my Telesthesia on that night and your mind will be attuned to mine." The letter also warned him to avoid all alcoholic beverages. At the appointed time, he did as he was told, sitting in front of a lit candle in a candleholder he had purchased from the Church of Love, and focusing all his thoughts on images of the Angels and Mother Maria. For all of the next day, Blanchard said, he experienced a great and inexplicable feeling of "joy."

After taking part in the Circle of Love, Blanchard was asked to contribute to something called "The Sacred Fire of Chonda-Za," a ceremony where "six vestal virgins" each lit a ceremonial candle. The ritual followed the rules of "an ancient myth." When each candle was nearly extinguished, a new candle would be lit in its place. All of this, of course, required money. Later, a letter came for Blanchard telling him that a special ceremony had been enacted with the lighting of the first candles: "Mother Maria lit the fire. You were with us in spirit and we saw your image in the flames and we all knew the ritual was as much for you, darling, as it was for us."

As Blanchard's involvement with the Church of Love grew deep, some letters from the Angels began referring to him as "the chosen one." These usually accompanied appeals for him to help build Chonda-Za, which Blanchard understood to be "a valley paradise where eventually the Angels, Maria and the male members of the Church of Love would live." Chonda-Za increasingly became the focus of fund-raising letters Blanchard received—the Angels needed money to buy the land and start construction. In one letter, Mother Maria described the sacrifices she had made to bring her dream to fruition. "I am not certain that I, or anyone else, was put on this Earth for any particular purpose," she wrote. "I created my own unique purpose for living, as all should do. My vowed purpose is to create Chonda-Za, the new Garden of Eden. I see no other purpose to my life. So it is I devote all of my mind, my abilities, my energy to the realization of my goal. There can be no other way for me."

"There is but one obstacle yet to be overcome," Maria wrote, "a Love Offering most grand, most generous." Blanchard ended up sending in enough money that the Angels bestowed him with a title that he would one day hold at Chonda-Za. A certificate naming him a "Temple Master" soon arrived in the mail, accompanied by a list of secret vows. It was the highest rank a member could hold and granted him authority over a temple in the future utopia.

The eventual disintegration of the Church of Love hit Blanchard hard. In court, he testified that he really did believe he was going to live out his days in Chonda-Za as a Temple Master, and that he looked forward to being "well-treated with respect at all times." When he found out that the Church of Love was being disbanded, he was crushed. "I felt like the bottom had been pulled out from underneath me," he said.

The trial in Peoria ended just a few days before Christmas, 1988. The jury found Don Lowry and Pamala St. Charles guilty of fraud and money laundering. In keeping with the many operatic twists in the case, right before they were to be sentenced they both disappeared from Illinois, setting off a national and international manhunt.

Lowry and St. Charles first fled to Montreal. Eventually, they made their way to Florida. Two months after they fled Illinois, they were tracked down by marshals in the Palm Beach suburb of Lake Worth, where Lowry was posing as "the Reverend Norbert Gaines."

The marshals caught him when he showed up at a postal box to collect money sent to him by members of the Church of Love who believed he was the victim of a witch hunt. Lowry was extradited to Illinois, where he received a sentence of twenty-seven years in prison.

After serving ten years and receiving parole, Lowry made his way to Butler, Pennsylvania, where he had spent the formative years of his childhood and where I eventually tracked him down to arrange an interview. When I arrived, I found that the bustling, World War II–era city of Lowry's youth had disappeared. Like so much of the Rust Belt, the main street was hauntingly empty, lined with sad, shuttered shops. Industries that once propelled the city's growth had dried up or moved away. The grand, mid-sized town that had once existed had vanished. In its place was a town in disrepair, with steep unemployment and a drug problem so bad that the city would later erect an "overdose memorial."

Lowry was in an old, rundown, tan house, with a big backyard he seldom used. Before my visit, I had only seen one picture of him, taken when he was still a young man. He was handsome then, with a narrow nose, and piercing, intelligent eyes. He wore his moustache pencil-thin and neatly manicured, making him look a little like a young Walt Disney. But the man who greeted me at the door was frail, rail-thin, and bald. He was eighty-two years old but looked like he could have been much older. (Lowry died in 2014, just a couple of years after our interview.) The interior of the house was shabby and in disarray. Ashes were strewn about his desk, and the whole house smelled of pipe smoke. He had had a great baritone voice, the kind made for old-timey radio. But a lifetime of smoking had left him so raspy it was sometimes difficult to follow what he said.

The interior of the house might fairly have been described as a museum to the Church of Love. Far from wanting to forget, it seemed that all Don wanted to do was to remember his glory days running the organization. Cabinets overflowed with old Angel love letters. Press clippings were strewn about the room. There were hundreds of photos of the models who once posed as his Angels.

The most interesting mementos were an assortment of old Church of Love knickknacks—such as flower vases and candelabras that bore Mother Maria's likeness. Around these he had scattered the little copper coins he had once distributed to members. On one side of the coins, "Chonda-Za" was etched in large letters, with "Hillsdale, Illinois" printed underneath.

We talked about the heyday of the Church of Love, the years Don spent writing letters; of being the puppet master of a rich and fictional world. "I loved it," he told me. As my voice recorder ran, I asked him to read an excerpt from a memoir he had written: "Quite a few members were intelligent enough to accept the Angels for what they were: fictional characters," he said. "But the majority absolutely refused to believe that the Angels were anything but honest-to-God real live girls. Members loved the Angels. They said the letters from the Angels gave them something to look forward to, and the Angels made them happier than they had been for a long, long time. Picture a short, fat, bald man in his fifties who lives alone and who hasn't had a date with a girl since his wife divorced him or died several years ago. He is bored, drinks too much, unhappy, and terribly lonely. Then Angels come into his life. Beautiful young girls who think he's a great guy, who like and respect him, who gladly accept him for who and what he is."

Initially, Lowry said, he had included "fine print" disclaimer language that described the letters as a fantasy. But he dropped that language, he said, when it became clear to him that members paid no attention to it. "They believed what they wanted to believe. They would just scan it, [and say] 'oh, he's just saying that to protect himself.' And they'd go on believing in the Angels." I pointed out to Lowry that his allowing the members to believe the fantasy was extremely lucrative for him. "Even those who knew it was a fantasy, they sent money," he countered. "And many of them, during the trial, stood up and said, 'I knew it was a fantasy. But I loved it.'"

In the course of the interview, Lowry sometimes painted himself as the noble creator of a social services program. Other times, he acknowledged that he had made a rich living off the credulity of his marks. "Looking back now, did you do something wrong?" I asked. "I think I did something very wrong," he said. "Because I should've kept that disclaimer in the pitch for membership." But I pointed out that he had just said that members blew off the disclaimer—it made no difference to them. Lowry agreed the disclaimer would likely have done little to sway the beliefs of die-hard members, but said that it would have afforded him legal protection.

This, of course, is along the lines of what many video games and online services do today. When you sign up, you are asked to scroll through a dozen pages of legalese that few people read, and even fewer understand. (I once did a story for NPR showing how little time people spend reading "terms of service" agreements. One study found volunteers were perfectly happy to click "Agree" even when the fine-print language included ridiculous terms such as giving up a first-born child as a condition of accepting the agreement.) Once you click "Agree," you are legally saying that you understand that what is about to unfold is a fantasy. Thereafter come many modern versions of the Church of Love. You can build a city, play first-person shooter games, run a farm. You can have avatars that wander into virtual worlds, and fall in love. You can spend hours and hours immersed in these worlds. Some people emerge into the "real world" after spending time in these online communities and feel hoodwinked and cheated. But the vast majority emerge feeling happy. Outsiders might mock you, but you are happy to have been seduced into experiencing the thrill of being a warlord, or crushing a neighboring farm, or dominating a galaxy far, far away.

More than three decades have passed since Joseph Enriquez received his last letter from Pamala. Time has changed the city of Dalhart. The once-vibrant downtown, anchored by a beautiful Spanish-style courthouse, has dried up, giving way to sprawls of businesses lining the interstate highways, including an inordinate number of cheap motels that cater to passing motorists and the crowds that descend on the city for the annual XIT Rodeo and Reunion.

Joseph Enriquez lives in the same house he lived in when he received his first letter from the Church of Love. It is just a stone's throw from the house where he was born. The neighborhood features lots of brown yards and dogs, with chain-link fencing and corrugated aluminum sheets separating one yard from the next. Joseph's house is weathered and long overdue for a new coat of paint.

Inside, the house is cluttered with old furniture, some of which was built by Joseph's late father, and filled with books and pamphlets about Christianity, astrology and Tarot cards. Zodiac symbols, which Joseph describes as good luck charms, hang over the front door. Pictures of Joseph's parents sit on a shelf that dominates the living room, along with a small statue of the Virgin Mary. A devout Catholic, Joseph still faithfully attends Sunday mass at St. Anthony's of Padua, the church where he attended parochial school.

Now in his sixties, Joseph is a small man, slight of build, with straight black-brown hair hanging below a Denver Broncos cap. His dog Chewbacca—his only true companion—is usually by his side. Several years ago, complications from diabetes prompted doctors to amputate some of Joseph's toes, and this left him with a slight limp. He still has a youthful naivete, an impish glimmer in his eyes. He speaks softly, with gentle earnestness.

Signs of Joseph's relationship with Pamala still adorn his house. He has seen all the news reports, and knows most of the details of Lowry's fraudulent operation. Yet he still treasures the mementos he received from Pamala. A pebble she sent him as a token of her feelings is in his bedroom. The lighthouse figurine sits prominently atop his dresser, where he can see it when he goes to sleep at night and when he wakes in the morning. Next to the lighthouse is a photo of Pamala, with her Farah Fawcett hairdo. She is holding her poodle, Gigi.

Joseph has had a lot of time to reflect on his relationship with Pamala. He harbors no bitterness or anger. He looks back at the Church of Love with a mixture of nostalgia and yearning. Nothing can sway him from the conviction that his involvement with Pamala was a life vest that kept him afloat during a hard period in his life.

"We have a dream that we're going to find someone we're going to be in love with and you're going to live with forever and everything is going to go on a perfect path and a bunch of daisies and flowers and butterflies," he says. The Church of Love "kind of gave us that feeling." Pamala was what he was looking for, a woman who was "actually interested in you, not what you have in your bank account, the house you have, the car you drive and stuff like that."

Pamala, he says, "gave me a chance to talk to somebody. I was pretty downtrodden. She just told me to hang in there, and when I was down to my lowest feeling, she'd tell me flat out, 'Get on your feet again.'" That's the kind of feeling he still gets from the picture, and the lighthouse. "I know it's not much," he says. "But it *means* so much . . . Every time I get up I look at it. I do that, I look at the lighthouse, and I go into the master bedroom of the house, where my mom and dad's pictures are. I look at them. And even though things are rough, you gotta have faith."

PART III
The Tribe

8

||||||||||||||||||||||||||||||||||||||||||||||||||||||||||||||||||||||||||||||||||||||||||||||||||||||||||||||||||||||||||||

Walking through Fire

*There are no gods in the universe, no nations, no money, no
human rights, no laws, and no justice outside the common
imagination of human beings.*

Yuval Noah Harari, *Sapiens*

The self-deceiving brain shapes our personal lives in innumerable ways. It influences our search for meaning—for companionship in the face of loneliness, for comfort in the face of illness. It
shapes the way we interact with brands, and it governs many rules
of interpersonal communication. When we ignore its directives, it
doesn't go away quietly. It springs back with a vengeance to under-
mine the plans and goals of the rational mind. It insinuates itself
into our relationships, and reshapes our perceptions of reality. Its
greatest power, however, is not in the way it shapes our individual
behavior, but in the many ways it bends us to the call of our communities and tribes. The final chapters of this book explore this idea
in three domains—the pervasiveness of rituals, the rise of nations
and the enduring power of religion.

You might ask how mechanisms inside individual brains have
anything to do with the collective behavior of ethnic and religious

groups, or entire communities and countries. At the simplest level, groups are made up of individuals, and patterns of behavior among individuals manifest themselves at the level of groups. But at a deeper and much more important level, our individual brains—which superficially seem to belong only to us—are also wired to serve the larger needs of our groups. Some of this has to do with the way natural selection works: If you remember the idea that each of us is a "survival machine" for our genetic information, then it stands to reason our genes would sculpt our brains to ensure not only our personal well-being but the well-being of others who are like us. Our genes, after all, don't live just inside of us. They live inside our fellow tribesmen and tribeswomen. Natural selection has of course endowed us with a powerful drive to survive, and to look out for our individual self-interest. None of us would throw away our lives lightly. But there are special subroutines in these algorithms: If I were to sacrifice my life for the well-being of my tribe, and thereby ensure the genes inside of me live on in future generations, you would predict such behavior would be "selected" and conserved over thousands of generations. Reason might tell you it doesn't do you any good to be dead. But in special circumstances, the self-deceiving brain makes you willing to prioritize the needs of your group over your own rational self-interest. Rituals, nations and religions offer windows into this idea.

In the aftermath of the Rwandan Civil War, groups of Hutu militants fled across the border into the neighboring Democratic Republic of Congo. Many villages fell under their control. Those that they did not control were often the targets of their brutal raids. The Congolese village of Bulambika found itself in a particularly bad spot. It was situated in the province of Sud Kivu, where Hutu forces were concentrated, and where the bloodshed was widespread even by the standards of the region. Rape was so common that the United Nations Assistant Secretary-General for Humanitarian Affairs declared the area around Bulambika to be "the worst in the world" in terms of sexual violence. There was little the local people could do to defend themselves. The villagers were farmers. They only had machetes. The Hutu militia had guns and rifles— and lengthy histories of violence: Some of the same militants had carried out the genocide in Rwanda against the Tutsi. Things were so bad in Bulambika that people were afraid to work the fields and tend to the crops.

One night in 2012, after a particularly grisly raid on a neighboring village where Hutu militiamen killed and mutilated dozens of women and children, an elder in Bulambika had a dream. In it, he was visited by the spirits of his ancestors. They told him of a secret ritual that would enable him to build a charm to protect his people and defeat their enemies: The elder was to travel to a far-away forest. There he was to harvest special roots, plants and animal intestines which he would blend into a powder. This powder would then be placed in a *gri-gri*, a pouch typically used in Congolese charms. After the intended recipient underwent a special ritual, he would become invulnerable to bullets.

The idea of bulletproofing rituals has a long history in Congo. Some versions have held that eating a man's heart makes you bulletproof. The Congolese warlord Vita Kitambala was able to keep a grip over his fighters largely because of his purported ability to make his men bulletproof. He was also supposed to be able to bestow the power of flight and to make himself invisible.

A ritual that promises to make its practitioners invulnerable to bullets is based on a proposition that is easily checked—and easily falsified. Yet such rituals have proved remarkably resilient through history. What are we to make of them? Are they some kind of doomed collective psychosis that arises among peoples, societies and cultures threatened with extinction? Or is something else at play? Could a bulletproofing ritual actually *work*?

In 2015, the economists Nathan Nunn of Harvard and Raul Sanchez de la Sierra of the University of California set out to answer those questions by studying the bulletproofing ritual of the Congolese village of Bulambika. They arrived about three years after the elder's fateful dream. A reasonable person—that is to say, someone who has a healthy degree of skepticism in the ability of a magic ritual to curb the trajectory of a bullet—would suspect that things had turned out very badly for the people of Bulambika. But the economists were surprised to find that for the better part of two years, the villagers had been living in peace. The vicious cycle of raids by Hutu militants had ended.

Nunn and Sanchez de la Sierra learned that following the elder's dream and his "discovery" of the bulletproofing ritual, his *gri-gri* charm had been tested on a goat. The animal was fired upon, but survived. After that, the villagers embraced the ritual and the charm. With their courage buoyed by their newfound invulnerability, the young men of the village stopped fleeing at the approach of Hutu raiders. Instead, they steeled themselves with the ritual and fought bravely with the weapons they had available. Sometimes, village youths managed to kill their attackers and recover weapons from the militiamen. When the next raid came, the youths were now even better prepared.

Predictably, fighting the Hutu militants came at a high cost. Villagers were regularly killed. But these deaths were chalked up to individual errors in the correct implementation of the complex ritual. Over time, as word spread of the village's fearless defenders, Hutu militants began to reconsider their raids on Bulambika. They backed off, and the villagers received growing confirmation that their ritual and charm really worked.

Nunn and Sanchez de la Sierra concluded that belief in the bulletproofing ritual was the deciding factor in Bulambika's struggle for survival. As economists, they saw the villagers' behavior in terms of a cost-benefit analysis, where people could either stand and fight, or flee. Belief in the power of the ritual tipped the equation in favor of resistance, which ultimately saved the village from extinction. From a scientific perspective, the belief was false. Nonetheless, it resulted in survival.

Bulletproofing rituals are not unique to Congo. Such rituals are nearly as old as the firearm itself. Two of the most famous examples date back to the end of the nineteenth century. The first happened in the Great Plains region of the United States, during a period when war and American government policies were pushing Native American cultures to the brink of collapse. One day during a solar eclipse, a teenage Paiute named Wavoka had a religious vision in which he saw all the native peoples, living and dead, united in peace and harmony in a future paradise. Gradually, as his experience and his teachings spread through the tribes of the Great Plains, the teachings of Wavoka—who had mostly been raised by a family of white ranchers and had been christened Jack Wilson—evolved into a new religion, a blend of traditional Native American beliefs and apocalyptic Christianity, known by the name of the ritual practiced by its adherents: The Ghost Dance.

The Ghost Dance eventually found its way to the Sioux in the Midwest, where it blended with existing myths and morphed into a prediction: Sioux ancestors were to return with a great herd of bison to drive the white man back across the ocean. The Sioux introduced an important new element to the Ghost Dance ceremony: The Ghost Shirt, which was supposed to make those who wore it invulnerable to bullets.

The climax of the Ghost Dance movement came in the winter of 1890, at a creek in North Dakota called Wounded Knee. American soldiers herded about three hundred and fifty Sioux Ghost Dancers, mostly women and children, into a makeshift camp. When soldiers began ransacking Sioux tents in search of hidden weapons, a medicine man named Yellow Bird called on his people to resist, and assured them that "bullets cannot penetrate us." In the hail of gunfire that followed, as many as two hundred and fifty Ghost Dancers were killed. They were, in the words of one survivor, "shot . . . like we were buffalo." For their efforts, around twenty American soldiers were awarded the U.S. Medal of Honor.

After Wounded Knee, the Ghost Dance quickly faded away. But within a few years, another bulletproofing ritual emerged across the world in China, among a group called the Righteous and Harmonious Fists. The Boxers, as they were more commonly known, were drumming up nationalist resistance to foreign imperialism by incorporating various supernatural rituals into their rigorous martial arts training. One of their rites was a practice called the Armor of the Golden Bell, a ritual spell that was supposed to make participants invulnerable to bullets.

The rise of the Boxers was a response to heavy-handed European encroachment that included missionaries enticing thousands of Chinese to abandon their ancient practices, and to embrace a foreign religion. Eventually, the Boxers ended up at war with an international coalition comprised of all of the most powerful countries in Europe, plus the United States and Japan. As one might suspect, the Armor of the Golden Bell proved disastrously ineffective on the battlefield, and the Boxers were roundly defeated. The foreign coalition managed to occupy a large swath of central China, including the capital city of Beijing. A year-long occupation followed, marked by indiscriminate looting, rape and retaliatory murder.

In contrast to the experience of the people of Bulambika, the history of the Native American Ghost Dancers or the Chinese Boxers might look like failures. Both groups suffered humiliating defeats, after which their respective beliefs in the efficacy of bullet-proofing charms evaporated.

Yet the legacy of each episode is actually more complicated than it might seem. The Boxers may have lost the war, but the conflict marked a dramatic shift in the course of Western imperialism in China. Though the bullying of China by Western powers continued through economic means, the European countries no longer aimed for outright conquest. Today, many Chinese see the Boxer Rebellion as the start of a seismic shift from being a weak nation on the verge of dismemberment to an influential world power.

It's harder to see how the Ghost Dance may have been a plus for the Native American tribes that embraced it. By the time native peoples donned their Ghost Shirts, they were too outnumbered and outgunned to put up any real resistance against the might of the United States. Yet as Red Cloud, Chief of the Oglala Sioux, put it, the movement offered a chance to unite his people, and they "snatched at the hope." The name Wounded Knee remains a rallying call that has helped Native Americans maintain a sense of collective identity.

The *gri-gri* of the Congolese, the Ghost Shirt of the Sioux and the Armor of the Golden Bell of the Boxers all served a psychological purpose: Each helped a group muster resistance in the face of an existential threat. The outcome of this resistance varied, sometimes producing defeat and sometimes victory. But at the very least, the rituals were all "successful" in prompting group cohesion and collective action. Each produced tangible benefits at the level of tribe, nation and culture.

While bulletproofing is an extreme example of the vast array of ritual practices we see throughout the world, it provides important clues to why billions of human beings perform an array of seemingly senseless acts every day. Rituals encompass everything from hazing at university fraternities and the consumption of bread and wine at the Eucharist to shaking hands when we greet each other and celebrations by soccer players when they score a goal. The extreme circumstances in Bulambika showcase why rituals are so ubiquitous, and why they have often been preserved across generations: Rituals offer a way for human beings to deal with a dangerous and unpredictable world. They generate community, conformity and courage. Asking whether they "work" in a literal sense misses the point. They work at a *psychological* level, and sometimes—as in the case of the Congolese village that fought off the Hutu militants—psychological reality turns into actual reality.

In the Tsodilo Hills of northwestern Botswana, in a region the local San people call the "Mountains of the Gods" and the "Rock that Whispers," there is a cave that contains an image of a python carved out of the face of the rock. The python is a figure of great importance to the San. In their creation myths, humans are said to have descended from snakes—creatures that also shaped the surrounding hills in their never-ceasing search for water.

The archaeologists who first discovered the cave found few tools or other signs that it was used for any practical purpose, such as shelter. But they did discover a number of well-crafted Stone Age arrowheads that had, unusually among the San, been painted red. Many of the red arrowheads had been burned in a fire, leading some archaeologists to conclude that the burnings were sacrificial, and that the cave was used to perform rituals.

Although the exact age and nature of the site has been the subject of debate, some archaeologists have estimated it to be seventy thousand years old, which would make it the world's oldest known site for performing rituals. If true, that would mean human beings have been practicing rituals at least as far back as when the first groups of humans reached the far corners of Europe and Asia, at a time when people were first beginning to think abstractly and engage in symbolic behaviors.

The first edition of the *Encyclopedia Britannica*, published in 1771, described rituals as the "order and manner to be observed in celebrating religious ceremonies, and performing divine service." But rituals aren't necessarily religious. Atheists practice a dizzying array of rituals in everyday social interactions, such as greeting one another in formalized ways, or following a series of prescribed steps while hosting dinner parties. Rituals to mark momentous events like a college commencement ceremony or the swearing in of a country's new president can involve both religious and secular elements.

Americans do not think of themselves as a ritualistic people. Yet in 2017, American couples spent an average of thirty-three thousand dollars on their weddings. That figure doesn't include the cost of a honeymoon—which, of course, is another ritual. Even among the most destitute people in the world, those living off a dollar or less per day, investments in wedding and funeral rituals are often prioritized over food and basic necessities. One study found that among families composed of the poorest of the poor, half had spent money on weddings in the previous year, and at least fifty percent had spent money on religious festivals. In the Indian state of Rajasthan, ninety-nine percent of the poorest families in one district devoted money to religious festivals over the course of a year.

Aliens observing human beings would be mystified as to why Catholics kneel and cross themselves as they enter a church, or why quarterbacks in football point heavenward after throwing a touchdown pass. The pervasiveness of rituals is remarkable considering that one of their defining characteristics is that they serve no practical purpose. In fact, the point of a ritual is that *there is no obvious point*. This is why the presence of the burned arrowheads around the Tsodilo Hills python were a clue that they were used in rituals. Why go through the trouble of making an arrow only to burn it in a fire?

Some rituals have remained stable over centuries, or even millennia. The earliest known archeological evidence of a ritual burial, for instance, dates back around forty thousand years, in what is now Australia's Lake Mungo. A fifty-year-old man was painted with red ochre after death. His body was placed in the burial site with knees bent and hands interlocked over his waist, as if at peace. It isn't that different from the way a nonreligious family in North America might today bury a loved one. Rituals focused on purity, or the preparation of food, or the crowning of rulers, are strikingly common in far-flung places. Whenever you see the same behavior occur in different places, at different times, and among people who have had no contact with one another, it tells you there is something about the behavior that is likely woven into the fabric of the human mind.

Growing up in India, I often marveled that people would spend money on "pointless" rituals when their kids didn't have clothes, or when families couldn't afford books for school. Why did people mutilate themselves, or undertake painful pilgrimages, when they already had so much suffering in their lives? On a trip to Montreal, I observed devout worshippers climbing—on their knees—ninety-nine hard stone steps at St Joseph's Oratory in order to share the pain that Jesus experienced. In my twenties, these rituals struck me as bizarre and wrong. It's taken me decades to understand that people turn to such rituals *because* of poverty, sickness and other deeply felt needs: Rituals ward off anxiety, they connect us to our history and to our cultural moorings, they bind us to our groups. As we will later see, one of the surest ways to eliminate "meaningless" rituals is to *address the source of the threat* or to solve the problem that the rituals were invented to fight.

The significant demands that rituals place on participants turns out to be essential to their social and psychological utility. There are certainly rituals that involve limited costs, but many ask a lot of participants. Some involve enormous investments of time and effort, or mind-numbing repetition. Others require intense physical sacrifice. In Greece, Orthodox Christians perform a ritual called Anastenaria to honor Saint Constantine and Saint Helen by walking barefoot across burning coals. In the Philippines, Catholics enact a Good Friday ritual by having themselves actually crucified, their hands and feet nailed to crosses. In the Indian states of Maharashtra and Karnataka, Hindu and Muslim rural families sometimes participate in a seven-hundred-year-old practice of dropping their newborn babies from shrines onto carpets held by men dozens of feet below—a ritual designed to demonstrate piety and to bring the children good luck.

Before you dismiss these as examples of religious dogma, consider the secular hazing rituals so common in military barracks and frat houses. A ritual known as "crossing-the-line" was practiced in the days of wooden sailing ships to mark a sailor's first passage across the equator. Author William Golding, himself a naval veteran, described it in brutally stark terms in his Booker Prize–winning novel *Rites of Passage*: A man is violently abducted from his cabin and dipped half-naked into a "badger bag"—a vat of seawater and human excrement—after which he is humiliatingly paraded and forced to bow before an officer dressed as Neptune. Though the ritual has been toned down over the years, versions are still practiced in modern navies.

Notice that settings where hazing rituals are often most common—the military, sports teams and frat houses—are typically settings that place special emphasis on group bonding. Rituals are a powerful way to carve out an "in-group"—people who have been through an ordeal or unusual practice together—from the "out-group"—those who wouldn't understand. The social-bonding effect of rituals can be observed even when they are stripped of the powerful cultural contexts in which they are usually found. In one experiment, psychologists asked some subjects to engage in an arbitrary ritual they had created from scratch. One researcher, psychologist Nicholas Hobson, later explained the details to me: "Take the cup, fill it up with lukewarm water. Make sure that it's not too cold, not too hot. Place your coins so the smaller coin, like a dime, should be in your non-dominant hand, the larger coin, like a quarter, should be in your dominant hand. And we want you to carefully place that into the cup of water. Hold it, bow your head and continue on with these various sequences as they're laid out." It was clearly nonsense. Yet when the subjects were later asked to engage in simple games that would gauge their level of trust in each other, those who had been asked to complete the ritual demonstrated greater cooperation with other practitioners than those who had not. Interestingly, Hobson and his colleagues found that simpler variations of made-up rituals didn't "work." A certain level of commitment and complexity is needed for a ritual to be psychologically and socially effective. This may be why rituals often seem to become *more* effective as the burdens they place on participants become more intense.

When groups come together to perform a ritual, this can foster what the French sociologist Emile Durkheim called a "collective effervescence," giving participants a feeling of belonging and reassurance. Today, we might call this "social cohesion." Consider the extraordinary resilience of Judaism. Its dizzying array of rituals, and the fact that Jews have practiced them faithfully for centuries—sometimes in the face of genocidal persecution—have been important factors that allowed adherents to stick together and survive.

In recent years, researchers have uncovered lots of evidence for the group-strengthening effect of rituals. Many rituals are characterized by multiple individuals performing synchronized movements. One study found that the synchronized rowing of a college rowing crew led members to produce more endorphins than when individual crew members rowed alone. Besides alleviating pain and stress, endorphins are associated with social bonding.

All of us also engage in rituals in the absence of groups. These might have to do with the way we drink our coffee with a newspaper every morning, or the lucky shirt we wear for the big presentation at work. I have a special shirt I wear when my favorite football team faces a difficult game. Does wearing my shirt bond me with fellow fans? Possibly. But much of the time I'm watching the game on TV by myself, with no other fans around. The shirt obviously does nothing to alter the course of the game. So why do I do it? Well, it makes me feel better. In the face of uncertainty, the ritual gives me comfort. Again, asking whether this is only the illusion of comfort misses the point. I *know* my shirt does not affect the outcome of the game. But it *feels* like it does. It bolsters my hope, and allows me to engage in positive thinking. And that's the point.

The former Boston Red Sox star Wade Boggs, one of the greatest hitters in the history of baseball, used to take his batting practice every day at 5:17. Every day at 7:17, he did wind sprints. He exclusively ate chicken for his pregame meal, which earned him the nickname "Chicken Man." And before every at-bat he would sketch the Hebrew word חי, *khai* ("life"), into the dirt with his bat. (He was not Jewish.) Boggs had a well-earned reputation for being one of the most superstitious athletes in the world of American sports. But if Boggs was an outlier, he had lots of company at more moderate points on the scale. Michael Jordan famously wore his North Carolina shorts under his Chicago Bulls uniform for every game.

A range of research has shown that there may be method to the madness. Structured, repetitive behaviors can help to calm us down and to overcome anxiety. One study found that Israeli women living in war zones during the 2006 Lebanon War were able to reduce their anxiety levels by frequently reciting psalms. The same kind of soothing effects have been observed among Catholic students who recite the Rosary. By alleviating anxiety, rituals can help people perform tasks at a higher level. In another study, subjects were asked to sing Journey's "Don't Stop Believin'" using a karaoke program running on a Nintendo Wii. But first, half the participants were handed a piece of paper with these instructions:

Please do the following ritual: Draw a picture of how you are feeling right now. Sprinkle salt on your drawing. Count up to five out loud. Crinkle up your paper. Throw your paper in the trash.

Using the voice-recognition capabilities of the Wii, the performances of the participants were then evaluated by the program. Those who had been told to first perform the ritual reported experiencing less anxiety. More significantly, they also *performed* better by the objective criteria of the program.

Clinical surveys show that people often turn to rituals in times of emotional distress or trauma. Sometimes people come to rely on repetitive rituals so much that it tips over into pathology, as in the case of obsessive-compulsive disorder. As early as 1924, Freud remarked upon the striking resemblances between "neurotic ceremonials and the sacred acts of religious ritual."

Rituals are so hardwired into our makeup that we often don't realize when we are engaged in them. In one experiment, researchers first fitted their subjects with special sensors that would monitor their movements, as well as heart-rate monitors that would be useful in judging how much anxiety they felt. They then asked participants to prepare a speech about a decorative object that they would have to present to a panel of experts. After the subjects finished, they were asked to clean the objects about which they had just written. Using the motion sensors, the researchers were able to detect how much each subject's cleaning resembled ritualistic behavior. They determined this by rating the movements in terms of redundancy, repetitiveness and rigidity, all of which are characteristics of a ritual. The more anxious subjects were, the more their cleaning involved ritualized movements.

It's telling that the researchers used cleaning to measure ritualistic behavior. Ritualistic cleaning is one of the more common responses of patients suffering from anxiety disorders. But cleansing rituals are also among the most common rituals *in general*. Cultures and religions around the world have their own complex guidelines and proscriptions for how such rituals are to be carried out—everything from the Hindu practice of ritualistic bathing in the Ganges River to the *netilat yadayim* handwashing ritual of Judaism. In these practices we can see how two different psychological benefits of ritual—their power to strengthen our group-level bonds, and the comfort they provide to us as individuals—come together.

Ritual practices that involve extreme sacrifice offer some of the most revealing insights into the workings of the self-deceiving brain. Taking part in painful or difficult rituals—what experts call "costly rituals"—is particularly useful in *signaling our commitment* to groups, ideologies and causes, and in eliciting trust and commitment from others.

One study exploring this idea was conducted at the Spanish village of San Pedro Manrique, where Europe's largest annual fire-walk is held during the climax of the eight-day festival of San Juan. University of Connecticut anthropologist Dimitris Xygalatas and his colleagues used monitors to track the heart rates of both spectators and participants who walked across coals burning at one thousand two hundred and fifty degrees Fahrenheit. Remarkably, the researchers found that the heart rates of the firewalkers synchronized with their fellow participants, and even with onlookers. What's more, the researchers found that this synchronization was strongest amongst those who were separated by the least amount of what the researchers described as "social distance": The correlation was stronger if people knew each other, and even stronger between husbands and wives. Xygalatas observed that he and his colleagues "were able to predict people's social distance simply by looking at the similarities between their heart-rate patterns."

Another study took Xygalatas and his fellow researchers to the Indian Ocean and the island nation of Mauritius, where they observed what is perhaps the world's most grueling ritual: the Hindu rite of *kavadi,* a component of the Thaipusam festival that honors the god Murugan. Those who commit to the *kavadi* first spend ten days in fasting and prayer. This is just a warm-up to the real ordeal. Practitioners then engage in varying degrees of ritualistic skin-piercing, with some undergoing hundreds of piercings all over their bodies. It's not uncommon for large metal arrows to be inserted through the cheeks of participants. The worshippers then set out on a grueling five-hour journey, without food or water, over burning-hot asphalt. Some go barefoot; others wear shoes made of nails. All the while, each carries on his back a kind of mobile decorative shrine called a *kavadi*—literally, a "burden"—from which the ritual gets its name. The most dedicated drag a chariot that is attached to their bodies with hooks.

After one procession arrived at its destination, the temple of Murugan, researchers quizzed some of the participants. First, scientists asked their subjects about the extent of their pain and suffering, after which they were each paid two hundred rupees, a few dollars. Before they left, subjects walked through a tent where they had the opportunity to anonymously donate part of their earnings to the temple that honored the god Murugan. Those who had experienced the greatest pain donated the most. From a purely rational perspective, this doesn't make sense. But from a psychological perspective, rituals generate "prosocial," generous behavior. Extreme rituals are very effective at creating and building bonds between people, and getting individuals to place the needs of others over their own desires. In the case of the *kavadi*, those who had taken on the greatest amount of suffering felt the deepest connection to their community.

As a species, humans are not the strongest or fastest. We don't have sharp claws or teeth. Our muscles are puny compared to many other creatures. But what we do have is *each other*. Early humans learned this lesson over thousands of years of evolution. This is why the self-deceiving brain prompts us to band together, fight for one another, defend each other. It regularly overrules the logic of mere self-preservation because, in our evolutionary past, standing with the tribe increased the odds our genes would survive. Millions of people, many of whom know nothing of one another, can be bonded together through "meaningless" rituals into one fearsome superorganism. Today, the same psychological forces are what bind us together as Americans or Chinese or South Africans—they are the foundation of nations.

9

Something Worth Dying For

I only regret that I have but one life to lose for my country.

Attributed to Nathan Hale, hanged by the British for spying
for the nascent United States of America in 1776

E ach hour of every day, a sentry at the Tomb of the Unknown
Soldier in Arlington National Cemetery enacts an elegant ritual known as "walking the mat." The soldier—known as a "Tomb
Guard"—begins by marching twenty-one steps to the front of the
Tomb, turns to the east for twenty-one seconds, faces north for
twenty-one seconds. She then marches back the twenty-one steps
to her starting place, where she begins the ritual all over again. The
number twenty-one reflects one of the highest honors bestowed by
the U.S. military, the twenty-one-gun salute. The name of the ritual is drawn from the black mat that was installed because of the
indentations in the concrete caused by the constant repetition of the
ritual since 1937.

The Tomb of the Unknown Soldier sits on a picturesque hill-
side of Arlington National Cemetery, ringed by trees. The design
has the effect of channeling an onlooker's view across the Potomac
and into the heart of the nation's capital, Washington, DC. But

the monument itself—an eleven-foot-tall sarcophagus—is plain and unassuming. Even the inscription etched into its face is simple and unadorned: "Here rests in honored glory an American soldier known but to God." The understated words belie the fact that the Tomb of the Unknown Soldier is probably the most sacred symbol on the most hallowed ground in the entire United States of America.

Some three million people visit Arlington National Cemetery each year. Almost all of them stop by the Tomb of the Unknown Soldier. Many seat themselves on the steps of the adjacent Arlington Memorial Amphitheater, and enjoy a silent reverie that might fairly be described as religious. Those who take time to explore the Amphitheater will find on its walls this Latin phrase from the Roman poet Horace: *Dulce et decorum est pro patria mori*—"It is sweet and fitting to die for one's country."

The first to be buried at Arlington National Cemetery were four thousand Union soldiers who fell during the 1864 Battle of the Wilderness, the opening battle of Ulysses S. Grant's Overland Campaign and the beginning of the end of the Civil War. The number of graves has grown with each successive war. Today, some four hundred thousand veterans lie buried on the cemetery's six hundred and twenty-four acres.

What makes men and women willing to sacrifice so much for their country? For most of us, the answer is so obvious that it barely deserves consideration: We love our country, its people and its achievements. We admire its ideals and natural beauty. Not all of us might be willing to give up our lives for our nation, but almost without exception, we respect those who are willing to make that sacrifice. Many people would say their country represents something distinctive and great in the world. This is a particularly common view among Americans, who embrace the idea of American exceptionalism. For them, America is America because it *stands* for something—freedom or liberty or individualism or equality. This is true for Republicans and Democrats, rich and poor, recent immigrants and those whose families have lived in the United States for generations. I often get a lump in my throat when I hear a beautiful rendition of the national anthem or "America the Beautiful." These songs often remind me of my visit to Declaration House, the reconstructed home at the corner of Seventh and Market Streets in Philadelphia, where Thomas Jefferson drafted the Declaration of Independence. I remember reading the words he wrote and feeling tears brimming in my eyes: "We hold these truths to be self-evident, that all men are created equal . . ."

Asking Americans to think of America might bring to mind familiar tropes—that we are "a nation of immigrants," that we are founded on "Judeo-Christian values," or that we are "the land of the free." Most people who visit the Tomb of the Unknown Soldier could recite some version of these beliefs. Yet Arlington Cemetery itself serves as a reminder of how deeply held beliefs about our nations—universal among people of all nationalities—are mostly myths, built over centuries on more complicated truths. The land the cemetery now occupies once belonged to George Washington Custis, the adopted son of President George Washington. Like President Washington and many of America's revered Founding Fathers, Custis was a slave owner. He brought more than sixty slaves to work on his plantation, and to build a stately, Hellenistic manor house. Today, that slave-built manor serves as a memorial at Arlington Cemetery to Robert E. Lee, who led the forces that defended the institution of slavery during the Civil War.

After the Civil War, the cemetery grounds were used to house former slaves—or, as the literature produced for visitors refers to them, "freed slaves." To call someone a *former* slave emphasizes their slavery; *freed* emphasizes their emancipation. Of course, calling them freed also conveniently emphasizes the larger story of America as a land of emancipation, rather than the story of America as a land of human subjugation. The truth is that the United States was a slave-owning country far longer than it has been a country where slavery was abolished. English settlers brought the first slaves to the United States as early as 1619, less than twenty years after the first English colony was established at Jamestown. That house in Philadelphia where I cried as I read the immortal words of the Declaration of Independence? Years after my visit, historian Annette Gordon-Reed told me that even as thirty-three-year-old Thomas Jefferson wrote those words about "self-evident equality" in the summer of 1776, he was waited upon—*in that same house*—by a fourteen-year-old slave named Robert Hemings. Jefferson owned hundreds of slaves. He fathered several children with a slave. The architect of America's vision of itself as a land of equality owed much of his wealth and station in life to the institution of slavery.

Or take our founding myths about Christopher Columbus. The hagiography surrounding this Italian explorer has long been one of our treasured national stories. But Columbus, of course, "discovered" a continent where vast numbers of indigenous people had lived for centuries. Historian Andrés Reséndez, author of *The Other Slavery: The Uncovered Story of Indian Enslavement in America*, told me that when Columbus ran into financial trouble in 1495—this after the riches he expected to find in his voyages did not materialize, in part because he had stumbled onto a different continent than the one he was expecting—"he decided that one good way to pay for these costs was by sending some Indians back to the slave markets of the Mediterranean, in this case in particular, to Spain.

And they selected, out of close to a thousand Native Americans, the best ones, crammed them into these ships and shipped them back to the Old World." In the years that followed, the practice expanded—women and children proved especially valuable in the markets of Europe, since they could be forced to provide a range of domestic and sexual services.

If one of those proverbial "anthropologists from Mars" were now to visit Arlington cemetery, she might be forgiven for shaking her head in amazement: How did a country that subjected so many people to slavery, degradation and exploitation come to think of itself as a beacon of freedom and human dignity? The region where Arlington Cemetery now stands was once home to peoples called the Anacostank, Pamunkey, Mattapanient, Nangemeick and Tauxehent, all of whom were driven out or dispossessed in order to create "the land of the free."

The founding myths of the United States—like the founding myths of all countries—are not just everyday hypocrisies; they are *foundational* to the construction of the nation. Why? Well, just ask yourself this question: What is a nation anyway? Most of us would like to think our countries are more than just a set of arbitrary lines drawn on a map. We might point to things like shared culture, history, language or ethnicity. But note that what makes one nation feel like a nation often has little to do with what makes another nation feel like a nation. The things that make Japanese feel Japanese are different than the things that make Americans feel American.

For more than a century, writers and scholars have tried to come up with a universal definition of a nation. One of the first to try was the nineteenth-century French intellectual Ernest Renan. "What is a nation?" he once asked. "How is Switzerland, which has three languages, two religions, and three or four races, a nation, while Tuscany, for example, which is so homogenous, is not one?" The answer, Renan concluded, is that there is no clear-cut answer, at least none that reflects reality. "No French citizen knows whether he is a Burgund, an Alain, a Taifala, or a Visigoth," he said, referencing the tribes that once flourished on the geographical boundaries of modern France. We think we are citizens of a nation because we have "forgotten many things."

Since Renan, others have tried and failed to establish a good definition of a nation. There really aren't any objective criteria that can explain the diverse origins, functions and commonalities of different nations. Perhaps the most accurate definition of a nation was put forward by the political scientist Benedict Anderson. His conclusion was that we believe ourselves to be Greek or Syrian or Nigerian simply because *we believe* ourselves to be Greek or Syrian or Nigerian. A nation, he wrote, is a social construction—an "imagined community."

All nations are collections of stories—stories about a shared past, stories we pass on about our heroes, and stories of failure, cowardice or cruelty that we ignore or suppress. Inventing stories, spreading stories and suppressing stories are all important, especially if you want to inspire someone to volunteer for military service, or to devote her life to civic purpose. Shared narratives are crucial when a natural disaster or a terrorist attack strikes one part of a country, and we want people in other regions to help. Why should a poor Texan help a homeless Californian when they share no blood ties, no business relationships, no common interests? It's because both believe they are part of the same nation, bound together by history, even destiny. The stories of nations prompt us to act as if we were one large entity, instead of hundreds of millions of individuals. "Two Serbs who have never met might risk their lives to save one another because both believe in the existence of the Serbian nation, the Serbian homeland and the Serbian flag," Israeli historian Yuval Noah Harari has written. "Yet none of these things exists outside the stories that people invent and tell one another."

Of course, the needs and priorities of nations change over time. So it should hardly be surprising that the stories of nations also change. Abraham Lincoln was progressive for his time, but he didn't believe in the equality of the races, and once said he would keep every slave a slave if it was necessary to save the Union. His initial ideas about emancipation sound a lot like immigration hard-liners today—Lincoln wanted to free slaves by deporting them "to Liberia, to their own native land." After the Civil War—and his assassination—Lincoln morphed into the "Great Emancipator." Is this whitewashing history? Maybe. But this new story about Lin-coln helped the civil rights movement make radical changes in the 1960s, and helped all Americans embrace what Lincoln once called "the better angels of our nature." The Rev. Dr. Martin Luther King Jr. chose to give his famous "I have a dream" speech in the shadow of the Lincoln Memorial in Washington, DC. Barack Obama chose Springfield, Illinois—the birthplace of Lincoln—to launch his his-toric campaign to become the first African American president of the United States. Whenever the modern Republican Party gets accused of racism, party stalwarts remind people that they belong to "the Party of Lincoln."

National myths can be semi-truths or outright lies. They can be versions of invented or imagined reality. But once invented—and once millions of people collectively believe in them—they *become* real. The philosopher Slavoj Žižek has said of these kinds of big, collective lies, "If everything is a fake, this fake, precisely insofar as we know it's a fake, tells us so much about the social reality in which we live. Even if it didn't happen, it's true."

The distortions, illusions and self-deceptions needed to create a nation serve an extraordinarily useful function. Our collective national fictions give us a shared sense of identity and purpose, the cohesion to accomplish great things, the will and the capability to defend ourselves against mortal threats. Without a sense of ourselves as a nation, we would never have commerce or currency or the rule of law. We could not generate revenue through taxation; we would not have a volunteer army. Without subscribing to the *story* of America, Americans would not have banded together to defeat fascism in World War II; they could not have built great works of public infrastructure such as the Hoover Dam or developed the technologies that took the first human beings to the moon.

As we have seen, illusions, myths and false beliefs can sometimes play a functional role in our lives. The myths underpinning the nation-state are among the most dramatic of these examples. These self-deceptions are responsible for creating some of the crowning glories of human civilization.

Standing amidst the gravestones in Arlington National Cemetery, a rationalist might ask why men and women are willing to give their lives for something that is, at root, an arbitrary set of lines drawn in the ground by other human beings. There is nothing sacrosanct about such lines—as evidenced by the fact that national borders change all the time as nations dissolve and new ones take their place. But the rationalists miss something important. Without the *story* of the United States, you wouldn't have Neil Armstrong walking on the moon, you wouldn't have Apple and Google, and you wouldn't have the New York Yankees or the Philadelphia Eagles. Just as the village of Bulambika would not have had the benefits of peace without believing in a fanciful story about a magic charm, without the story of America you wouldn't have all the practical, functional things that the United States offers its citizens.

Now, no one in their right mind would give their life to build a spacecraft, or for a Silicon Valley entrepreneur to build an internet company. To get all the useful things that nations provide their citizens, you can't just present a cost-benefit equation. Rational calculation doesn't prompt people to leap between a speeding car and a child, any more than it prompted the heroes buried at Arlington National Cemetery to give their lives fighting wars in distant foreign fields. "A man does not have himself killed for a half-pence a day or for a petty distinction," Napoleon Bonaparte once said. "You must speak to the soul in order to electrify him." In order to bridge the impersonal functional benefits of a nation with the very personal sacrifices needed to build that nation, you need to harness the powerful drives that human beings possess to act in the service of things greater than themselves. It's difficult to see how this works in a country like the United States, where myths and stories are now centuries old and have been woven together into impenetrable knots. It's easier to see how it works by looking at new nations—and the people who try to construct them.

In 2016, a video began making the rounds on the internet. It featured a handsome, Middle Eastern–looking man in his early twenties who spoke perfect English. His name was Ahmad Sami Kheder. The video was professionally composed but not slick. It looked like it was produced by a small, nonprofit organization that was looking for doctors willing to work in a war-torn, developing country. Here was footage of Kheder working next to high-tech medical equipment; Kheder tending to newborn babies at a hospital; Kheder pointing out parts of the human anatomy on a diagram of a human torso as a roomful of students looked on. He always had a stethoscope draped over his shoulders like an unwound scarf, which made him seem simultaneously hip and authoritative. He was usually smiling.

Toward the end of the video, Kheder directed a missive to his fellow Muslims in Britain. He delivered it with a disarming earnestness, and his voice was peaceful and calm:

> *I don't want money. I've never been interested in having a big house, expensive cars, this isn't the life I wanted to live. And* hamdallah *I found a great cause. And I ask you all to join this cause, to join in helping all the Muslims here. All the ones, the brothers who are putting their lives on the line for you and to raise the words of Allah . . . Please, open your eyes, and make* hajj *to this land, where people are fighting for Islam, not fighting for democracy, not fighting for political gains. Everyone needs to ask the question here, where do I want to stand? All the people in England, I ask you again. All the Muslims over there,* taqwallah, *leave the land of England and come here to make* hijra *here in* wilayat al-khayr *and in* Dawlat al-Islam . . . *There is a great cause being fought here, and the caravan is leaving. And I hope* inshallah *I will see you all here.*

The most significant element of the appeal was his casual reference to *Dawlat al-Islam*, Arabic for Islamic State. The video was actually an ISIS recruitment pitch, one aimed at Western medical students and doctors who had the technical skills and training that the terrorist group desperately needed. Kheder, who would later be killed in the battle for Mosul, had himself been a new recruit just a few years before the video appeared. He made the decision to join ISIS while attending medical school in Sudan, where he had family roots. He had crossed into Syria to join ISIS along with nine other British students from the university. All were in their late teens or early twenties, and three had already received their medical degrees. Later, more foreign-born students from the university followed.

The Sudanese university began desperately looking for ways to stem the tide. Eventually, an administrator reached out to Scott Atran, an anthropologist affiliated with Oxford University, the University of Michigan and the French National Center for Scientific Research. Atran's fieldwork has earned him a reputation as one of the world's leading experts on the motivations of jihadi militants. Later, I spoke to Atran about that phone call. He recalled that the Sudanese administrator was flummoxed. "They were our best students," Atran recalled the administrator saying, adding that the parents of the students were "hysterical."

What made the situation bewildering was that the students seemed utterly unsuited to joining a terrorist outfit. Kheder was a native of the bucolic, upper-middle-class London suburb of Carshalton. He once attended a posh grammar school, where he had at one point been a straight-A student. A friend described him to a British newspaper as "decent, smart, cool and outgoing—never the kind of person who would be speaking or encouraging the idea of jihad or terrorism." Another said he "seemed to enjoy all the vices that supposed Western decadence had to offer." He had never showed any signs of being particularly religious. A photograph taken in 2009 captured him holding a can of beer and standing in front of an English fast-food establishment as he celebrated his exam results.

Newspaper accounts of the other students recruited by ISIS described them in much the same way. Like Kheder, most came from upper-middle-class families. Few seemed religious. Many were active on social media, leaving digital footprints that weren't different from those of other British teenagers. A profile of one of the students noted that he had four hundred and eighty Facebook friends, and liked the band Coldplay and *The Fresh Prince of Bel-Air*. Another had five hundred and forty-six friends, and liked Manchester United, Beyoncé and the television show *Boondocks*. These were not poster children for a terrorist outfit that beheaded its victims.

But Atran wasn't surprised by the way the young men were described. He had spent a long time in Iraq and Syria interviewing and studying captured ISIS militants, as well as al-Qaeda–affiliated Nusra Front soldiers and the Kurdish Peshmerga soldiers who had fought against them. His research showed that, contrary to the conventional picture, ISIS militants were driven by factors more complicated than most people imagined. Religion was often an afterthought among the Western-born supporters who flocked to join ISIS. Atran's fieldwork is supported by data from the countries from which recruits were drawn. Statistics from France showed that eighty percent of French ISIS recruits came from families described as "nonreligious." Other data found that the typical ISIS recruit is "born again" to religion only *after* they have committed to the group's mission.

Would-be ISIS revolutionaries were often drawn from groups that felt marginalized. ISIS expertly exploited their feelings of inadequacy or inferiority, Atran said, with messages that appealed to "the idealism, the adventure, the search for glory, the desire for change" inherent in young people: "They take each of these personal stories, which they'll invest hundreds of hours in, and try to show why my personal frustration, your personal frustration, at this moment in your life, it's not because you couldn't get this job, or that you failed in this, or your team lost, or whatever. The reason that happened, you see, is because of this larger set of factors, of this larger world set of forces that have been arrayed against you, of which this is just a trivial part. And forget about the trivial parts that are affecting your life. Go now and deal with the real causes of the unhappiness, not only of you but of people like you around the world, the oppressed."

This kind of storytelling and myth-making might fairly be described as propaganda. But Atran said it is not that different—psychologically speaking—from the stories and myths that have propelled other revolutions, such as the Bolsheviks in Russia, or the firebrands of the French Revolution. Many world-altering movements have relied on the power of leaders to tell a convincing story of past glory, present suffering and future greatness, a story about wrongs that need to be redressed. These stories can harness something very powerful among followers, especially those from disaffected groups: They can prompt people to make great sacrifices for what Atran and other researchers call "a sacred cause."

A sacred cause is something that gives people a sense of higher meaning and purpose, the feeling that they are devoting their lives to something larger than themselves. It can be like fighting for a "holy land." But it can be secular, too. In his research on combatants in Iraq, Atran found that ISIS fighters, who were willing to fight bravely on the battlefield, had a high level of devotion to their cause. But he also found that Kurdish Peshmerga forces, the only local combatants in the region capable of standing up to ISIS, also showed extremely high levels of devotion to *their* cause, rooted in national aspirations and Kurdish identity—what they call "Kurdeity."

Obviously, a group like ISIS is a very different beast than an existing country like South Africa or China. But studying upstart groups like ISIS shows us something that is harder to see in established nations—the extent to which their creation relies on myth-making and storytelling. Few "Italians" could even speak what we now think of as Italian when the Italian state was first created.

Napoleon Bonaparte made himself the embodiment of France, but spoke French with the thick accent of his native Corsica. The principal differences, psychologically speaking, between the "country" that ISIS briefly founded and more established nations in the world are how widely its myths were adopted, how successful these stories were at harnessing followers, and how long the self-deceptions lasted.

I once asked a linguist what the difference was between a dialect and a language. "Languages," he quipped, "are dialects that have armies." Myths are like that, too. When they start out, when they've just been invented, they look crazy and incoherent. You might laugh at them. But allow them to settle in for a few generations, get several million people to believe them, teach them in your schools and textbooks, glorify them in your songs and movies, back them up with guns and armies, and, voilà, they become the foundational building blocks of a nation.

The Republic of Kurdistan was a pipedream twenty years ago. Today it doesn't sound so far-fetched. Fifty years from now, if the dreams of Kurdish nationalists materialize, and the Kurdish national anthem is streamed to the world at the Olympics as Kurdish weight lifters accept their gold medals, we might wonder how there could ever have been a time when the nation of Kurdistan did not exist. The commitment of ISIS fighters and the Kurdish Peshmerga are examples of how our minds yearn for sacred causes. Once such causes have their claws in us, they can enlist us to serve ideologies, religions, and what Atran has termed "the quasi-religious notion of the nation."

"This is not just true for the Islamic State," Atran said. "This is true for people who are willing to sacrifice their lives and kill others at the same time across the board. And it's also true for movements that are peaceful, but where the people who are driving these movements are willing to shed their own blood—for example, the civil rights movement or movements like Gandhi's movement in India. They are committed to a set of values which are sacred. That means values which are immune to trade-offs. For example, you would not trade your children or your religion—probably—or your country for all the money in China. And when you have these kinds of values, which you will not trade off and which are not subject to the standard constraints of material life, things that occurred in the distant past or in distant places that are sacred are actually more important than things in the here and now."

Atran's research has shown that Islamist soldiers under the grip of a sacred cause begin to fuse their individual identities with those of the group. "Once this happens," he said, "they develop a sense of invincibility and actually perceive themselves—their own bodies—to be much bigger than they are."

Sacred causes—and the myths and stories that underpin them—give us something to value beyond our own lives. They can be the fuel that prompts soldiers to fight to the death on the battlefields of Normandy, or induces suicide bombers to blow themselves up in Kabul. There is, of course, no moral equivalence between the two acts. But at a psychological level, people willing to lay down their lives for a cause have much in common.

Subsuming our lives in the service of our tribes and nations can yield a form of immortality. When we fuse our individual identities with our groups, we become larger than just our individual selves. Even after we die, we live on through others who belong to the same groups. This is reflected in the way all cultures remember their fallen heroes. In 1935, Adolph Hitler gave a speech in which he memorialized sixteen followers who were killed during his unsuccessful 1923 "beer-hall putsch." Hitler said the men had attained "German immortality" and that "the dead of our Movement, Germany and its men, living and dead, live on." Similar language can be found in almost all countries. U.S. president James Garfield once praised fallen soldiers for having "made immortal their patriotism and their virtue." In Russia every year, people march with photographs of relatives killed in World War II as part of what are called "Immortal Regiment marches."

Foundational national myths, while useful in the creation of groups and nations, also regularly produce catastrophe. In 1944, for example, the Nazi war machine faced a dilemma. The Normandy Invasion in June of that year had brought the Allies to Germany's doorstep. With the United States and Britain attacking from the west and Russia from the east, German military leaders saw disquieting signals that the war effort was going very badly.

When military leaders requested that every last resource of the German state be focused on its challenges on the battlefield, Hitler and the Nazi leadership demurred. Nazi leaders insisted that precious resources be diverted from the war effort to transport Jews captured from the countries that Germany had conquered to concentration camps. Exterminating the Jews, Nazi leaders felt, was not just as important as winning the war; the war *could not be won otherwise*. As Marvin Perry and Frederick M. Schweitzer explain in *Antisemitism: Myth and Hate from Antiquity to the Present*, Hitler overruled his military experts:

> *Common sense also demanded that one does not murder people whose labor could be utilized for the war effort. Yet despite the protests of some high-ranking officers and officials in the army and the armaments industry, the SS sent Jewish workers, many of them skilled, to the death camps, and when Germany's military plight was des-*

perate, the SS still diverted military personnel and railway cars to deport Jews to the gas chambers of Auschwitz. They did this in defiance of common sense because they viewed the annihilation of the Jews as a prime war aim that warranted their total commitment.

Beliefs that Jews were evil—that they were a central cause of Germany's decline after the First World War, that their extinction was essential to the success of Germany—these were among the foundational myths of the Third Reich. In 1944, Nazi propaganda chief Joseph Goebbels noted, "In the case of the Jews there are not merely a few criminals (as in every other people), but all of Jewry rose from criminal roots, and in its very nature it is criminal. The Jews are people like no other people, but a pseudo-people welded together by hereditary criminality . . . The annihilation of Jewry is no loss to humanity, but just as useful as capital punishment or protective custody against other criminals."

The lesson here is that national myths can be powerful even when they are completely unhinged. The Nazis are an extreme example, but it is easiest to see how myths work when we look at groups that we abhor. (In general, it's easy to see the delusions of our opponents for what they are, and very hard to see the myths of our own groups, teams and nations with clear eyes.) The Nazi example is also instructive in that it shows how the same myths that underpinned the creation of Nazi ideology, that allowed Hitler to come to power, also helped to destroy the Third Reich.

Why didn't Hitler let go of myths about the Jews even as destruction stared him in the face? Even mass-murdering psychopaths have the capacity to be rational, to act in their self-interest. Surely, the rational thing for Germany to do in 1944, in the face of looming catastrophe, was to focus entirely on the war effort? But the reason foundational myths are powerful in the first place is that they are resistant to rational analysis. Put another way, nations come into being and endure for years, decades or centuries because of the *stability* of their foundational myths, the ability of these stories to withstand skepticism, challenge and doubt. Of course, if the functional upside of enduring myths is cohesion, such myths also come with a downside—they can keep nations from changing and adapting in the face of radically altered circumstances.

When asked to choose between annihilation and giving up their myths about the Jews, the Nazis chose annihilation. Surely it was because their myths did not appear to them to be myths, but eternal truths. They had convinced themselves and millions of Germans that their theories about the Jews were true. National myths have the power to construct nations because they *seem* like immortal truths—black-and-white answers in a world filled with gray. Change may be inevitable, but stability requires us to believe that change is impossible.

Our minds are vulnerable to myths, falsehoods and fictions not merely because we are dumb or stupid, but because we are frail, flawed and easily afraid. Advocating fearless rationality—an end to myth-making and myth-believing—is not just about being smart. It is a matter of privilege. If you don't lack for food and water, for physical security or a police department that comes when you call, you might not feel the need to turn to myths, rationalizations and rituals. You may have no need for fellow members of your tribe to come to your assistance when you are sick, because there are doctors and hospitals who will do a better job. If you think of yourself as a citizen of the world because borders are illusions and people everywhere are the same, you probably haven't lived through the kind of persecution that makes you desperate for the protection of your fellow tribesmen. It's fine to hold secular, cosmopolitan views. But when rationalists look down on people who crave the hollow panaceas of tribe and nation, it's like Marie Antoinette asking why peasants who lack bread don't satisfy themselves with cake. They fail to grasp what life is like for most people on the planet.

People gain a sense of meaning and purpose when they submerge themselves in the myths, stories and rituals of their tribes. In the face of impermanence and loss, our groups remind us that a form of immortality is within reach. When we make sacrifices for sacred causes, we know we will be remembered in places such as Arlington National Cemetery. The beliefs that underlie nations might fairly be described as illusions. But the nations in which we live, which we call home—whose accomplishments make our hearts swell with pride and whose national anthems fill our eyes with tears—these would not exist without such self-deceptions.

In the future, should nations no longer be the principal way people organize themselves on the planet, it's a safe bet we will develop new stories and myths to make whatever systems we come up with seem like eternal truths. As I have tried to show in different ways, the forms that groups take—tribes, nations, alliances—these change all the time. What underlies them all—and what will outlast them all—is our capacity to invent myths, to believe in them, to fight and die for them.

It's worth remembering that the nation-state is itself a relatively recent invention. Long before we had national boundaries and national flags and national anthems, groups of humans still needed to band together to aid one another and to confront enemies. Then, as now, the human desire to be part of something bigger than just ourselves helped to ensure survival.

10

|||||||||||||||||||||||||||||||||||||||||||||||||||||||||||||||||||||||||||||||||||||||||||||||||||||||||||||||||||||||||||||||||||||||||||||||||||

The Grand Delusion

A great book, therefore, is in part an act of deception, a tissue of lies: a trick. Indeed, it plays the fundamental human trick of finding or discovering, or imposing, meaning in the senseless, pattern in chaos, fish and princesses and monsters in the heavens. That act of deception is at root a self-deception, conscious and unconscious, and without it life would be—life is—a terrible, useless procedure bracketed by orgasm and putrefaction.

Michael Chabon, in the foreword to
Lewis Hyde's *Trickster Makes This World*

The Valley of the Kings lies beneath a towering, pyramid-shaped peak known as the Horn, at the intersection of the two very different natural features for which Egypt is known: To the east of the valley is the Nile and its lush, life-sustaining delta; to the west, the vast expanse of the Sahara, stretching on like an endless, lifeless sea. The juxtaposition of life and death makes this a fitting location for the resting place of Pharaohs, a symbolic border between the living and the dead.

The Egyptians, as the Greek historian of antiquity Herodotus once noted, were "religious excessively beyond all other men." This reputation stemmed primarily from their obsession with the after-life. The safekeeping of eternal souls was big business in ancient Egypt, and the priestly caste constructed an enormous industry based on magic spells and charms, ritual gear, secret knowledge and funeral rites. Ensuring immortality was a matter of great concern to all of Egypt, but especially to its rulers.

For centuries, the Egyptian Pharaohs erected massive pyramids to serve as burial chambers. But these proved notoriously vulnerable to grave robbers—it was as if each bore a huge neon sign saying, "Here lies treasure beyond your wildest dreams." So the Pharaohs eventually turned to the valley—barren, inconspicuous and conveniently close to the ancient capital of Luxor—and built their tombs in secrecy, underground.

The first tomb was built in the Valley of the Kings in the sixteenth century BCE. Over the next five hundred years, the valley became a kind of royal graveyard, with each new generation striving to eclipse the tombs of the last in size and grandeur. Eventually, the valley became the final resting place of Ramesses II, the greatest ruler in the history of what was then the greatest civilization the world had ever seen.

Ramesses II's conquests had expanded Egypt's borders, bringing ruin to its enemies and unimaginable riches to its people. At home, he was a prolific builder, initiating public works projects on a scale the country had never known. The most important was his own tomb, the largest that would ever be built in the Valley of the Kings: A labyrinthine, multilevel structure of at least one hundred and thirty rooms (possibly as many as two hundred) where the Pharaoh was interred along with many of his fifty-two sons. At the time of his burial—before centuries of grave robbers and flooding took their toll—the rooms overflowed with all kinds of ostentatious wealth: gold, jewels, marvelous works of art. But they were also stocked with all manner of mundane, everyday items: vats of wine and beer, clothes, perfumes, weapons, even mummified food. Three thousand years later, those things would seem out of place in a grave. But for the ancient Egyptians, they were a necessary part of a proper burial. The afterlife, for them, was not altogether different from the world through which the Pharaoh had just passed. Death was not an end, but simply a transition to a new world, one where food and wine and weapons would all find their use.

The story of this transition is told in great detail in Ramesses II's tomb, in intricate, colorful hieroglyphics painstakingly carved into the walls and onto the bits of pottery and clay tablets that have survived centuries of calamities. These were drawn from the various books produced by the ancient Egyptians to describe what happens to one's *Ka*—essentially a soul—after death. The most important of these books was what the Egyptians called the "Book of Coming Forth by Day," which European explorers would later come to call the Book of the Dead. Portions of the book meticulously copied onto the walls of Ramesses II's tomb involved the steps the Pharaoh needed to take to arrive safely in the world of the afterlife. It was a guidebook, filled with useful advice for navigating the many challenges that would have to be overcome, eventually culminating in the Pharaoh's judgment, when his heart would be weighed on the scale of the goddess Ma'at.

This concern with the afterlife extended to the most famous of the ancient Egyptian burial practices—mummification. After death, one's *Ka* was imagined to periodically return to one's body. Ramesses II's well-preserved mummy is a particularly good example of the skill and care that went into protecting a royal corpse. Three thousand years after his death, he looks remarkably good for a man who lived to ninety, with a narrow face and a handsome hooked nose. He still has a fair bit of hair, red from the ritualistic dyeing that took place after his death, which rings a top shorn bare like a medieval friar's tonsure.

Ramesses II's quest for immortality did not end with the preservation of his earthly remains. He also went to great lengths during his life to ensure his legacy. The great buildings and temples he constructed were often accompanied by detailed reliefs recounting his heroic deeds and achievements. He had countless statues of himself erected—often on enormous scale. One of the largest of these was a thousand-ton depiction of the ruler as a young man at the Ramesseum, the vast temple complex he built adjacent to the Valley of the Kings. A portion of this statue, shipped to Britain in the nineteenth century, became the inspiration for one of literature's most famous meditations on the futility of the search for immortality, Percy Bysshe Shelley's poem *Ozymandias*—the name the Greeks gave Ramesses II:

> *And on the pedestal, these words appear:*
> My name is Ozymandias, King of Kings;
> *Look on my Works, ye Mighty, and despair!*
> *Nothing beside remains. 'Round the decay*
> *Of that colossal Wreck, boundless and bare*
> *The lone and level sands stretch far away.*

An obsession with the afterlife is not unique to ancient Egypt. Every religious tradition holds some sort of belief about our fate after we die. As far as we know, religious beliefs have existed in every culture and every society. For centuries, philosophers, writers and scientists have delved into the question of why religion exists, and how it became so pervasive in the human world. Karl Marx saw religion as "the opium of the people." Sigmund Freud once called religious belief "a universal obsessional neurosis." Richard Dawkins and members of the "new atheist" movement describe religious faith as "delusions."

Addictions and neuroses and delusions imply sickness or dysfunction. But these terms don't help us understand why religion has exerted such a huge sway over human affairs for thousands of years. Some thinkers see the pervasiveness and staying power of religion as evidence of its *functionality*. In recent decades, a number of researchers have proposed that religions came into being because they served many deeply felt human needs. One influential school of thought along these lines is called *terror management theory*. It's based on the idea that for much of human history (and for many people on the planet today) the world—perceived realistically—isn't pleasant or meaningful, but depressing (when it isn't terrifying). Humans, perhaps uniquely among all creatures, understand that they are mortal and that death is inevitable. This, according to terror management theorists, produces incapacitating fear. Humans have adapted to such fear by turning to a variety of mental defenses, some of which involve invocations of supernatural forces.

We can see shades of terror management theory as far back as the first half of the twentieth century in the ideas of the psychologist Otto Rank, who ascribed religious belief to "our will to live forever—colliding with the immutable biological fact of death." But the basic tenets of the idea are usually traced to the 1973 Pulitzer prize–winning book *The Denial of Death* by the anthropologist Ernst Becker. Becker painted a view of humans that was at once horrifyingly real, and horrifyingly depressing. We might want to think of ourselves as ethereal, spiritual, high-minded creatures. When we hang our important diplomas on the wall, or buy fancy cars, or dress ourselves up in fine clothes and jewelry, we seek to show the world our status and communicate our high view of ourselves. But this view sits in defiance of reality: We are embodied creatures, intensely dependent on food and water, vulnerable to disease and injury, and fragile in the face of aging. Every aspect of our daily lives offers a screaming reminder: Without this gulp of air, this piece of bread, this sip of water, you are steps away from death and decomposition.

Social psychologist Sheldon Solomon stumbled onto Becker's book during a visit to the library. He found himself captivated, and became one of the principal architects of terror management theory. In Solomon's words, every human being is really a "breathing piece of defecating meat." But you can't go around thinking of yourself as a breathing piece of defecating meat. It gets in the way of happy hour. It isn't the right frame of mind for office meetings and graduation ceremonies. So what to do? In the face of the facts, Solomon and his colleagues Jeff Greenberg and Tom Psyzczynski argue, we come up with convenient fictions to distract and comfort ourselves. We become masters at managing our terror because to do otherwise is to invite incapacitation.

The neuroscientist V. S. Ramachandran has gone so far as to speculate that our inability to deal with the ever-present awareness of death is why our capacity for self-deception evolved in the first place. Self-deception, he wrote, developed as a "psychological defense mechanism . . . a coping strategy for avoiding fear of death." Human beings who could avoid existential dread by employing denial, illusion and self-deception—who weren't, in Ramachandran's words, "paralyzed by the constant fear of death"— had an evolutionary advantage over humans who could see reality clearly. Self-deception became functional.

The idea that our innate fear of death can exert such a huge sway over our lives might sound like theoretical musing, not the kind of claim that lends itself to experimental testing. But terror management theorists have produced an impressive amount of experimental evidence to back up their ideas. Researchers have published more than five hundred papers that offer empirical support for the theory. Most involve manipulating what the theorists call *mortality salience*, the psychological term for a person's conscious awareness of death at any given time. The death of a loved one, for instance, can have a long-lasting impact on mortality salience. Watching a television show in which someone is killed could also impact your mortality salience, but for a shorter duration and to a smaller degree.

The results of these studies suggest that the fear of death shapes human behavior in ways large and small, and not just in ways that are overtly religious. For instance, death reminders lead us to become more generous toward those who share our cultural and political beliefs, and to act more harshly toward those who challenge them. In one experiment, two groups of subjects were asked to read articles by professors that were supposedly published in the scholarly journal *Political Science Quarterly* (they weren't). The first article—by a supposedly pro-U.S. author—noted some of the United States' weaknesses, yet concluded that America was "a great place to live freely." The second—by an anti-U.S. author—concluded that "the idea that the U.S. is a promoter of world democracy and freedom is a total sham." While both groups responded more favorably to the pro-U.S. article, those who had first been reminded of their own mortality showed a distinctly stronger bias. Similar studies have shown the same results in other cultures. When Germans were interviewed about their taste in cars, food and vacation destinations, for instance, they tended to favor German products and locations more when the interviews were conducted in front of a cemetery compared to when the interviews were conducted at a storefront.

Sometimes, death reminders prompt people to adhere more strongly to social norms—whatever their culture deems to be "good." Solomon believes this is because in the face of threat, it is comforting to fall back on the "certainties" of one's group or culture. You may be mortal, but your culture, your group, lives on after you—it offers a sort of immortality. Judges in Arizona who were first reminded of their mortality imposed harsher penalties on sex workers than judges who were not reminded of their mortality. The difference was significant: When asked to evaluate the behavior of women who had violated cultural norms, death-fearing judges imposed sanctions that were *nine times larger* than judges who did not have death on their minds. People reminded of death also awarded more generous *rewards* to people who performed prosocial, or culturally approved behaviors. In both cases, it is as though people reminded of their own deaths hew to actions that defend their culture's norms—they are more willing to reward culturally sanctioned behavior and to punish culturally deviant behavior.

Some terror management studies have found the fear of death can have impacts that are difficult to anticipate. Israelis who thought of themselves as good drivers drove *more* recklessly when they were reminded of death. Divers took longer and more dangerous dives when asked to think beforehand about their own mortality. Sunbathers exposed themselves longer to the sun when informed about the risks of cancer. What was going on? In each case, groups hewed more strongly to things they identified with—the Israeli drivers to their driving, the divers to their dives, the sunbathers to getting a tan—when reminded of their own fragility. Markers of identity function like the cultural touchstones we discussed earlier—they offer a mental defense against terror. Ironically, if the actions of people in these groups reduced their terror about mortality, it likely increased their actual risk of death. These studies offer insights that have applications to policy: To discourage people from smoking, for example, we mandate that warnings about smoking's ability to kill be placed on cigarette packs. One study, however, found that among people who gain self-esteem from smoking—think rebellious teenagers who imagine smoking makes them look cool—reminders of the mortality risks posed by cigarettes raised their mortality salience and paradoxically *increased* their desire to smoke.

The impact of death-awareness on our cultural attitudes can be seen even among young children. In one Israeli study, seven-year-olds were asked to rate their willingness to befriend Israeli-born or Russian-born children. Half the group was first asked a variety of questions about death, such as "Will every man die at some time?" Being reminded of death made seven-year-olds react more negatively to all the photographs, but there was no difference between the way they saw the Israeli children and the Russian-born. On the other hand, when the same study was conducted on eleven-year-old Israeli children, those who were first asked questions about death showed a distinct bias in favor of Israeli-born children.

Philosophers have also grappled with questions of self-deception in the context of death and dying. Stephen Cave talks about a "mortality paradox": We understand that we will one day die, but we cannot really imagine being dead. When we think about being dead, we are simultaneously playing the observer and the observed—someone who is not dead imagining what it is like to be dead. This is such a challenging idea that many of us simply avoid thinking of it: The Indian epic *Mahabharata* says one of the great paradoxes in the world is that we know that all people will die, but we never believe that it will be our turn next. Put simply, our minds are not designed to intuit nonexistence. The Spanish philosopher Miguel de Unamuno described the problem succinctly: "Try to fill your consciousness with the representation of no-consciousness and you will see the impossibility of it. The effort to comprehend it causes the most tormenting dizziness."

To get around the problem of the mortality paradox, Cave argues that humans have invented a series of self-deceptions that he calls "immortality narratives." The first of these might be described as the longevity story: the belief that through potions or herbs, fountains of youth, magic elixirs or hidden knowledge, we can extend our lives, perhaps indefinitely. The ancient Egyptians had schools of magic devoted to staving off threats to health. Many religious texts and mythological stories tell the tales of people who lived far longer than humans today. Adam of the book of Genesis, for instance, supposedly lived to nine hundred and thirty. Bhishma, a great Indian warrior in the *Mahabharata*, was said to have the power to choose the moment of his own death. Some religious traditions, such as Daoism, teach that longevity can be extended to the point of achieving immortality right here on earth.

The second immortality narrative that Cave has identified is the one emphasized by the Abrahamic religions: Resurrection. If it isn't possible to live forever in your current body, no matter. After death, your body can be revived, and you can live on again. Not only is the resurrection of Jesus central to Christian theology, Jewish and Muslim traditions both tell of a future day where true believers will be resurrected in a heavenly afterlife.

Since the first two narratives run into logical and philosophical conundrums—when we look around, we don't see people living forever, and no one has ever seen someone come back from the dead—the third immortality narrative takes a different tack. It ignores the physical body altogether. It suggests that even though the body may be mortal, we have an essence that lives on forever—a soul. Buddhist and Hindu traditions take this a step further and suggest that, after death, our souls transmigrate into new bodies—we are reincarnated.

The fourth immortality narrative involves coming up with ways to live on forever—not in one's own body, not in one's own body that has been resurrected, and not through one's soul—but in a *figurative* sense, as a memory in the hearts and minds of other people. It's about leaving a legacy, like the one Ramesses II sought to create. Even those of us who do not build thousand-ton statues of ourselves hope to live on through the legacies of our good deeds, our children—and the groups, societies and nations that will outlive us.

The immortality narratives fit perfectly with terror management theory. Religion, like culture and nationalism, can provide us with a bulwark against the fear of death. Various studies have demonstrated this idea. When people who believe in the afterlife are confronted by death, they tend to believe in it *more*. In a series of interviews conducted with soldiers who had returned from combat in World War II, many frequently recounted memories of situations where the fear of death was accompanied by a heightened belief in God.

This is not a new revelation, or particularly controversial. Deathbed conversions are an old phenomenon. One of the most popular stories in the English language, *A Christmas Carol* by Charles Dickens, describes the conversion of the miser Scrooge, employing one of Stephen Cave's immortality narratives. Scrooge changes his ways and becomes a generous and helpful person because he is afraid of death. As Scrooge recognizes his own looming mortality, he does exactly what volunteers in psychology studies do—he seeks out the solidarity and the approval of his community through prosocial acts, and he seeks to cement his legacy through acts of generosity.

Scrooge's story is instructive in another way: It shows how some immortality narratives do more than just soothe our fears. They also get us to behave in ways that an economist might say are anti-thetical to our "rational" personal interests, but that are valuable to the interests of our groups and communities. This idea lies at the core of a second powerful theory to explain the ubiquity of religion around the world.

As human societies grew beyond small bands of hunter-gatherers, they encountered many new problems. When groups were tiny, every person was likely to know everyone else. If some-one stole from you, or treated you badly, you would know to steer clear of that person in the future. Others would take note of such behavior, too, and the transgressor might be punished or ostra-cized. As groups grew in size, it became harder to enforce unwrit-ten norms through personal mechanisms, because there were many people who were strangers to one another. As individuals traveled outside their groups for trade, people came into contact with ever more strangers and found that the old ways of doing things didn't work anymore.

There was a second problem. For a long period in early human history, groups were extraordinarily egalitarian. This was not because people were socialists, but because there were few ways to accumulate wealth. If you killed a bison and decided to hoard all the food for yourself, you would only get a few meals out of your kill before the meat went bad. It made more sense for you to share the meat with others, to buy yourself goodwill in the expec-tation that, down the road, your neighbor might consider sharing her surplus with you. As groups grew larger, things changed: It became easier for people to act in antisocial ways and escape cen-sure. Strangers could cheat you, and you would not have recourse to a community of elders to settle matters. The rise of agriculture also made it possible to hoard wealth, and people began to act more like the economic actors we see in modern life. Since there were few formal systems of government to regulate how people interacted with one another—and whatever systems of government that arose were likely ineffectual or impotent by modern-day standards—the breakdown of the old ways was a harbinger of problems for many communities.

The collapse of group cohesion and solidarity would have been disastrous when it came to the proper use of scarce resources, such as water or grazing grounds. When individuals care only about their own well-being, things can go downhill very quickly. Of course, when this happens, both the rich and the poor can get taken down. Extinction for some can turn into extinction for all.

Researchers such as the psychologist Azim Shariff argue that these new challenges set the stage for the invention of an important *social* innovation: religion. Where interpersonal ties and tribal norms once ensured that people looked out for one another, religions now stepped in and told people that if they didn't play nice, there would be terrible consequences—either in their present lives or in the afterlife. Shariff points to a number of experiments that show that the fear of an angry, supernatural God is an extremely effective stick to get large numbers of people to treat each other properly and to act ethically. One of Shariff's studies (delightfully titled "Mean Gods Make Good People") gave students a math test and an easy opportunity to cheat. Afterwards, students were asked to rate the God they believed in on fourteen traits, ranging from "forgiving" and "loving" to "vengeful" and "angry." Those who believed in an angry, vengeful God turned out to be much less likely to cheat.

These kinds of experiments and field studies from around the world prompt Shariff and other researchers to hypothesize that this is why religions with punitive gods likely arose in the first place. Consider the Abrahamic God of Judaism, Christianity and Islam.

He is about as punitive as One can get. He punished inequity by wiping out nearly everyone on the face of the earth in a great flood, and all but two of every living creature. As societies grew in size, what Shariff calls "big, omniscient punitive Gods" helped enforce civic virtue, and provided a unified set of rules. They allowed for vast trade networks based on trust. A Muslim from one end of Asia, for instance, could trade with a Muslim at the other end, and each could be comfortable that their trading partner would not be a cheat because they both feared that the same God would punish them if they acted dishonorably.

Of course, this theory comes with its own set of challenges. How exactly did societies create angry gods and religions? It's not enough to say that such gods produce functional benefits. How did they come about in the first place? As we have seen elsewhere, the cost-benefit language of rational persuasion isn't likely to have produced the evocative myths and stories that lie at the heart of religions. It wasn't like early humans held a big meeting and decided they needed a new system to enforce the rules, and that they should start believing in punitive gods. No, religions likely arose in the same way that many of our biological features arose, through a process of trial and error. Different bands of people had different cultures, and some cultures had proto-religions. Just as animals that are better adapted to their local environments outcompete animals that are less well adapted, groups with religious beliefs outcompeted groups that did not have such mechanisms to enforce group cohesion and solidarity. In turn, as religions made some groups more successful than others, the religions of successful groups spread to conquered lands.

Beliefs that were functional—that yielded survival and success—were more likely to be passed down. For example, think of the biblical mandate to be fruitful and multiply. You can see how such a mandate would be functional over time. If you have lots of children, you increase your numbers, and eventually, you can conquer or subjugate groups that are smaller and weaker. Might some religions have recommended universal chastity or sexual abstinence? Possibly. But it isn't hard to see why such religions aren't around anymore. It also isn't hard to see why many religions in the world are fixated on questions related to the regulation of sex and sexual behavior. Shariff and others call the evolution of religion a form of "cultural selection," drawing on the analogy of natural selection for biological traits.

Religious beliefs also provided shared moral codes—a Constitution before there were constitutions. The atheist intellectual Christopher Hitchens was fond of saying that there is no moral behavior a believer could perform that one cannot imagine a nonbeliever performing. That is undoubtedly true. But that doesn't mean religion isn't a very effective way to get large numbers of people to follow a moral code. Religion is certainly not a prerequisite for morality, but the fact that religions are ubiquitous suggests that they have been a highly effective system to get people to act in ethical and benevolent ways—just like the miser Scrooge in *A Christmas Carol*.

Take the *azaan*—the simple but elegant Arabic call to prayer called out five times a day in Islamic countries, with its sing-song repetition of *Allahu akbar*—"God is great"—and the admonition to believers, *hayya ala-s-Salah*—"come to what is good for you." There may be more to this call to prayer than simple therapeutic ritual. One study conducted in Morocco began by giving shopkeepers a small amount of money—enough to purchase a few rides in a taxi. The shopkeepers were then asked if they would like to immediately donate some or all of the money to charity. While all the shopkeepers were generally quite generous with their donations, those who took part in the experiment as the Muslim call to prayer was heard in the background were even more willing to fork over their money to charity.

A similar study conducted in Canada borrowed a common technique from experimental economics called "the dictator game." The game tests generosity by giving people a sum of money and then asks how much they would like to share with a second person they will never meet who is sitting in another room. The "dictator"—the volunteer initially given the money—shared more than twice as much with their partner after being primed to complete word scrambles that featured the words Spirit, Divine, God, Sacred and Prophet. This was true regardless of whether the subjects described themselves as atheists or religious believers.

Religion has also long been used as a tool to mobilize people for war. For most of human history, this was extremely functional. Societies organized around religions that could call for war—a *jihad*, a crusade—had a cultural-evolutionary advantage. Soldiers inspired by religion were more likely to defeat their enemies than those who were not. It is no accident that German soldiers in World War II were issued belt buckles inscribed with the words "God is on our side." In a way, it isn't that different than the bulletproofing rituals of the villagers in Bulambika.

One of the most important insights that arises from these theories has to do with something we touched on earlier: The role of religious rituals. Elaborate and painful religious rituals, in fact, provide a mechanism to understand the entire concept of religion-as-social-innovation. Why would religions demand that people throw babies from shrines, climb stone steps on their knees, or mutilate themselves with nails? Why would religious texts celebrate fathers willing to put their own children to the sword when supposedly commanded by God? Well, think about the converse: What would happen if religions *didn't* impose extreme demands on believers? If the rise of religions fostered social cohesion—I trust you because we both belong to the same faith, and that faith requires each of us to treat the other properly—then this provides all kinds of incentives for one of us to cheat. Instead of actually *being* religious, I can merely *say* I am religious, and obtain all the benefits of group membership. I can reap the benefits of the club without paying any of the dues—I can free-ride. Costly rituals make free-riding difficult. If I merely want the benefits of religious affiliation, would I really be willing to undertake a costly pilgrimage or walk over burning coals? Probably not. On the other hand, if you see that I am willing to do those things, you can be fairly certain that I am indeed very religious. To put it another way, the more pointless the ritual, the more painful, the more valuable it becomes as *a signal of authenticity*.

A theatrical example of this kind of signaling in the animal kingdom is the peacock's tail. Male peacocks flourish a tail with beautiful feathers even though it slows them down and can make them vulnerable to predators. A flashy tail is a *signal* to peahens—the peacock is effectively saying, "I am so physically fit and healthy that I can survive even as I carry around this feathered monstrosity." Of course, none of this explicitly goes through the peacock's mind, any more than true believers tell themselves that they are walking over burning coals to send a signal of authenticity to other believers. Understanding how the mechanism works actually undermines its effectiveness. If you are a peacock, all you feel like doing—all your brain needs to tell you to do—is to strut your feathers. Peahens and mating bliss will follow. Your genes—and your propensity to flaunt a spectacular tail—get passed along. Similarly, if you are a devout believer, all you need to feel is that you are acting out the will of God. You don't need to understand the "why" of what you are doing. Shariff calls this "functional opacity"—the real reason the behavior exists is because it has a long history of successfully producing certain social benefits and ensuring group cohesion and survival, but practitioners are themselves in the dark about how their costly rituals might produce outcomes that benefit their groups.

The notion that religion is a force produced by cultural evolution, and that it primarily exists to produce functional benefits to individuals and groups can also explain why religions are *in decline* in some parts of the world. As human societies created nations, and devised mechanisms for self-governance, the punitive gods who were so effective at enforcing group norms and ethical behavior were no longer as necessary. Soldiers from diverse faiths could now be inspired to fight and die for the same country, instead of the same god.

Many religions once based on angry gods have morphed into faiths that talk about loving, forgiving gods—think of the difference between the Gods of the Old Testament and the New Testament. Nice gods might not provide the same glue of social cohesion, the same stick of ethical enforcement, but many societies today no longer need gods to provide cohesion and ethical guidelines—effective states and local jurisdictions are now perfectly capable of creating civic pride and enforcing ethical norms. As the necessity for the "keep-people-in-line" function of angry gods has waned, religions—especially in wealthy, industrialized countries—are increasingly providing a different suite of social functions via bake sales, childcare services and nonsecular versions of psychotherapy. They are still functional—they just serve different functions than they once did.

This can also explain why countries of the world with the best functioning states are also the places where organized religion has seen great declines, and why religious faith continues to flourish in places riven by poverty, inequality or social conflict. Scandinavians have lots of trust in their governments, excellent social services and high-functioning states. They also have some of the lowest levels of religious belief in the world.

We have looked at how religions help people manage the fear of death, and how they serve as an instrument of social cohesion. Religions also provide benefits in terms of individual health and well-being. Jane Cooley Fruehwirth at the University of North Carolina analyzed survey data tracking the health of adolescents in the United States. She found that religious adolescents appear to have better mental health than their nonreligious peers. Similar research along these lines has long elicited skepticism from atheists. Critics say such studies are correlational: they do not tell us which way the arrow of causation points. For example, religious teenagers usually come from religious households. If such households are more likely to remain intact because of religious proscriptions against divorce, for example, are the teenagers in better mental health simply because their parents are still together? In other words, is the apparent connection between religion and health a much more pedestrian and obvious relationship between family stability and health?

The best way to settle questions of correlation and causation is to conduct an experiment in which you deliberately change one variable and measure the effect of this change over time. Fruehwirth told me in an interview that conducting an experiment to settle this issue was out of the question. You would have to randomly assign teenagers to be religious or not religious and then track their mental health over time. You would have to force some religious people to become atheists and some atheists to become religious. Not being able to conduct such an impractical experiment, Fruehwirth found a clever way to test if the relationship was causal. She used something called *peer effects*: Religious teens are more likely to have friends who are religious, and depressed teens tend to have friends who are depressed. Such patterns of peer influence have been observed widely in many domains of human behavior. Fruehwirth used peer effects to eliminate some problems with earlier studies that sought to link religiosity with mental health: Since peers of religious teens were, in effect, made more religious at random—they just happened to be classmates with religious teens—this was a way to eliminate some of the confounding effects of family background and other variables. Fruehwirth found that even using this conservative standard, teens who became more religious as a result of peer exposure turned out to experience fewer mental health issues than teens who happened to have fewer religious peers.

Religion seems to exert a sway not only over our mental health, but over our health in general. Multiple analyses of obituaries in major cities across the United States have found that people who are members of religious groups live on average five years longer than those who are not religious, even when controlling for other factors that influence life span, such as gender and marital status. One study that recently looked at Des Moines, Iowa, found the difference in life span between believers and nonbelievers was ten years. If that number is to be believed, not going to church in Des Moines is roughly as risky as smoking.

People who regularly attend religious services tend to have greater social support networks, and larger numbers of close friends. They also volunteer more. These are all things that provide a host of health and community benefits. Critics of such studies— especially those who identify themselves as "new atheists" might scoff at findings that religion promotes longevity, saying that secular social groups that do not demand that people believe in fantasies could provide the same benefits. Yet other research has shown that clubs, amateur sports leagues or other large social networks simply don't have the same benefits provided by religious participation. Fruehwirth, for instance, found that teens who were part of debate clubs and sports teams did not see the same mental health benefits as teens who attended church regularly.

Religious faith might be the canonical example of how beliefs that are unprovable, or even demonstrably false, can sometimes be good for us. I do not for a moment mean to minimize the costs of religious dogma and fundamentalism. Many books have been written about the great costs of religious delusions. Few, however, have cared to tackle the thorny questions raised in these pages: What if false beliefs help people live longer and connect better with their families? What if myths help communities thrive? What if fictions allow nations to come together? What if self-deceptions prompt people to sacrifice themselves for the well-being of others, and thereby help their communities, tribes and nations?

As I said at the start of this book, I believe in the power of science, reason and logic. But a commitment to scientific evidence requires me to acknowledge that self-deception can sometimes play a functional role in our lives. This does not mean that we should embrace all forms of self-deception. What it does mean is that, if we care about the well-being of our families, our communities and our planet, we need to ask the hard question: When should we fight self-deception and when—and how much—should we embrace it?

Epilogue

To live on a day-to-day basis is insufficient for human beings;
we need to transcend, transport, escape; we need meaning,
understanding, and explanation; we need to see over-all
patterns in our lives. We need hope, the sense of a future.

Oliver Sacks, "Altered States," *New Yorker*

You probably remember the image from social media: A lone older Native American man is proudly singing a traditional song. He is surrounded by a group of rowdy, laughing white teenagers, some of whom appear to be mimicking tomahawk chops. One tall boy with a smug, disquieting smirk stares down the old man as they stand nearly face to face. The incident reeks of racism.

The social media controversy that came to be known as the Covington High School incident featured a group of students from a Catholic high school in Kentucky who were visiting the National Mall in Washington, DC, to take part in an anti-abortion march. The Native American man—a Vietnam veteran—was there for an Indigenous Peoples March. A minute-long video of the incident was posted on YouTube, and it ignited an uproar. The *New York Times* described it as an "explosive convergence of race, religion and ideological beliefs."

Julie Irwin Zimmerman watched the video like millions of other Americans. She found it "cringeworthy." In the few seconds it took to unfold, it crystallized for her everything she felt had gone wrong with the United States under the administration of President Donald Trump. The racism? Check. The bullying? Check. Julie's friends and social networks mirrored the way she felt: "I talked to a friend of mine who lives in New York, a former roommate of mine, and she said her yoga teacher called and said, 'let's drive to that school in Kentucky and protest.' Like, that's the sort of level of reaction people were having to this. Like, this yoga teacher in New York wanted to hop in the car and drive ten hours to protest in front of the school."

What brought the video home to Zimmerman, who is white, was that her own teenage son attended a Catholic high school in Cincinnati. If the teenagers in the video could do such horrible things to an elderly person of color, could her own kid or his classmates do the same? "I texted my son, and said, 'Have you seen this? I hope that you would never in a million years act this way in public,'" she said. She later told her son that she was particularly bothered by reports that the teenagers had been chanting "Build that wall!" at the elderly man. Her son listened. But then, soon after, he told her that he was hearing different accounts about what had happened from his friends. These accounts raised doubts about the version circulating on social media. Longer videos about the incident were soon posted on the internet. Zimmerman pored over these, hoping to prove to her son that he was wrong, that the chanting had taken place. Instead, she found that what had actually transpired was much more complicated than she had initially assumed. The Catholic high school students had first been accosted by members of a religious group called the Black Hebrew Israelites, who hurled insults at the boys. And the Native American man was far from being alone and outnumbered—he was with a large group of activists who were also actively clashing with the students. The original video had not shown any of this. And there was no chanting about "the wall."

Zimmerman found herself questioning her initial reaction to the boy with the smug smirk. "I don't know what he was thinking," she says. "I don't know what he was feeling. But I've seen that look on teenagers where you've got waves of thoughts passing through your head and your underlying thinking is, 'What do I do?'" Where she had once seen a "menacing" smirk, she now thought she saw nervousness and uncertainty. Zimmerman didn't think the teenagers were blameless. Some were behaving offensively. But the original video lacked context.

In an interview with me, she described her shifting feelings about the incident. She told me she felt she had done exactly what she tells her son not to do—jump to a quick conclusion based on preexisting biases and limited evidence. She had assigned blame before she even knew all the facts. Zimmerman is a writer. She used to work at the *Cincinnati Enquirer*. She filed a story about the evolution of her own thoughts for *The Atlantic*, admitting that her initial response had been hasty. Seemingly within moments, this "mea culpa" essay was circulated widely on conservative media. National Rifle Association spokeswoman Dana Loesch tweeted about it. Then Rush Limbaugh crowed about it on his radio show, which is heard by about fifteen million people per week. The subtext: A card-carrying liberal was finally coming clean, and admitting that liberals make up stuff, jump to conclusions about racism and believe the worst about their political opponents—even when those "opponents" are just kids.

For Zimmerman, becoming a poster child for the political right was difficult. "It's as though you're giving your enemy ammunition by admitting they might be right and you might have been wrong," she says. A part of her felt she had betrayed her own group, and that she had provided conservatives with a cudgel to bash her fellow liberals. She felt people in her own tribe looking askance at her. The whole thing was confusing: When she had leaped to a quick conclusion, shared her feelings with her liberal friend and amplified the outrage she felt, the satisfaction that comes with standing with her tribe—her fellow liberals—coursed through her. But when she slowed down, thought about things, looked for evidence that contradicted her opinions—and then was honest about what had happened—it felt like she was betraying people she cared about. How could it be that being truthful, honest and humble—the very lessons she preached to her son as virtues—had turned her, in the eyes of some allies, into a traitor?

"You saw this video and you had to pick a side without very much information," she says. "And if you were left-leaning, you were outraged by these kids, originally. If you were conservative, you just put your head under a rock because even you couldn't defend what you originally saw." But once the narrative shifted, it was conservatives who jumped up and said the story proved what they knew all along—that liberals played fast and loose with the truth. Many liberals whom Zimmerman admires refused to change course—they still blamed the teenagers for what happened.

"These events, these very symbolic events, are kind of touchstones," says Zimmerman. "You're either on this side, on this team, or you're on that team. And this is what I hate about our politics is that you can't explore any nuances or anything, you can't approach events as individual events. Everything becomes a fork in the road and you either decide you're on this team, you're with your people, or you're against them."

Around the same time that I interviewed Zimmerman, I stopped by a conference organized by the Association for Psychological Science in Washington, DC. The conference featured a panel on the psychological origins of conspiracy theories. UCLA psychologist Jennifer Whitson presented some findings that I thought perfectly described what happened in the Covington High story, as well as countless other social-media-driven uproars.

In a series of experiments, Whitson and her colleague Adam Galinsky found that when people experience a lack of control, they try to compensate for it using a variety of psychological mechanisms. "When individuals are unable to gain a sense of control objectively, they will try to gain it perceptually," the researchers wrote in a paper published in the prestigious journal, *Science*. Whitson showed volunteers a bunch of pictures, for example, some of which featured a recognizable image and others that just had random dots, like static on a television set. Volunteers saw images when they were present, of course, but those who were deprived of a feeling of control were more likely to imagine they could see images hidden in the static. Volunteers asked to remember a time when they lacked control also reached more eagerly for conspiracy theories—which, if you think about it, are a form of false pattern recognition. Volunteers in Whitson's experiments "saw" illusory patterns—just as Zimmerman reached for hasty and sweeping conclusions from the very limited information in the initial video, and just as conservatives leaped from Zimmerman's essay to draw sweeping conclusions about liberals.

The saga of the Covington High School incident is disturbingly familiar in many countries of the world today. What is less widely appreciated is how well psychological mechanisms involving self-deception and group dynamics explain why so many of us reach for unfounded theories, and why many of us are reluctant to discard them in the face of the facts. Zimmerman experienced this tension first-hand. She felt she had to make a choice between honesty and loyalty, between the tug of the rational mind that demands we seek out the truth, and the pull of the tribe, which demands we hew to the interests of our groups. Is it really surprising, in the face of threat and anxiety, that so many of us choose the imperatives of the groups to which we belong?

Jennifer Whitson's experiments showed there was a way to reduce false pattern recognition and the erroneous generation of conspiracy theories. It wasn't by hectoring volunteers with logic and reason, or by telling them that they were "morons" for subscribing to fantasies, but by addressing the problem at its *emotional* root—providing people with ways to boost their self-esteem and to restore their feeling of being in control. Paradoxically, we sometimes become more likely to listen to the voice of logic and reason when we *turn away* from logic and reason, and pay closer attention to people's unmet, underlying emotional needs.

This book has attempted to reveal a fundamental paradox in our relationship to the truth. Many intelligent people have come to believe—with near religious fervor—that reason and rationality constitute the highest good, and that these alone can produce the outcomes we want. As a card-carrying rationalist, I would love for this to be true. But as a card-carrying rationalist, I also need to follow the evidence where it leads. And the evidence (ah, the irony!) tells me that in many situations, we need to work with the self-deceiving brain even if—*especially if*—we want to achieve the goals of the rational brain.

Indeed, anyone who wishes to overcome the destructive delusions and self-deceptions that pervade our politics, our economy and our relationships would be wise to ask a new set of questions: What *psychological benefit* does holding a false belief confer on the people who hold it? What underlying needs does it address? Are there other ways to address those needs? If so, supplying those needs likely provides a powerful way to fight delusion and self-deception. Throwing evidence and data against passionately held false beliefs is important, but often futile. Many people hold false beliefs not because they are in love with falsehoods, or because they are stupid—as conventional wisdom might suggest—but because those beliefs help them hold their lives together in some way. Perhaps the delusion provides comfort against anxiety, or a defense against insecurity. Perhaps it draws the approval of their groups. Just as beliefs about an omniscient, angry God fall away when a functioning state provides us with infrastructure, laws and public safety, and when market economies provide us with consumer goods, entrepreneurial opportunities and good jobs, so also the way to root out self-deception is by compassionately asking what people lack, and exploring how we might help replace what is missing.

Along the way, we might also discover that there are some myths that we want to embrace, even foster. When we think of the present moment, in the early twenty-first century, our planet faces a terrible fork in the road. Humans are on the verge of triggering environmental catastrophe. The stock response of many scientists and science communicators to those who deny the existence of climate change is to belittle "deniers," to throw evidence at them, to tell them that "ninety-seven percent of scientists agree" that humans are the cause of climate change. But this is the language of the rational mind, not the self-deceiving brain. Such arguments can "make sense," but still end up being ineffective. To get results, you have to work *with* the algorithms of the self-deceiving brain, rather than ignore them.

Can you think of a powerful force that shapes the lives of billions of people in disparate parts of the world, in rich countries and in poor countries, a force that causes millions to act in the service of goals larger than themselves? Is there, perchance, some kind of *belief* system that gets people to place the needs of the collective above their own needs—that can turn the protection of our planet from a cost-benefit equation into a sacred value? Is it possible that religious faith might help us overcome one of the most staggering collective-action dilemmas we have ever faced in human history?

The new atheists will probably tell you that religion has no place in any solution for climate change. But as a pragmatist, I say we should care much less about what's true, and much more about what works. If believing in the Sun God or Shiva or the Abrahamic prophets can get people to stop destroying the only planet we have, I say we go for it. (For the 100th episode of *Hidden Brain*, I interviewed the Nobel Prize–winning economist Danny Kahneman. He told me, "For me, it would be a milestone if you manage to take influential evangelists, preachers, to adopt the idea of global warming and to preach it. That would change things. It's not going to happen by presenting more evidence. That, I think, is clear.")

Indeed, climate change is precisely the kind of challenge that religions may have come into being to solve: How do you get large numbers of people—most of whom are strangers to each other, and all of whom have strong incentives to look out for their self-interest—to work together in the service of the common good? Some religious people might be uncomfortable with using religion for practical goals. But I suspect many more would welcome the view that sees religious faith as uplifting and useful, rather than dogmatic and ignorant.

Think about the last time you read a great novel, a story that brought you to tears. When you finished the last chapter and closed the book, did you ask yourself if it was absurd that you shed tears over characters that were not real, over events that never really took place? Have you ever emerged from watching a great movie feeling cheated that your very real emotions were elicited by fictional events? Of course not. When I finish a great book or emerge from a theater after watching an amazing movie, the real world often feels less real than the world of the book or movie. If you asked me if the characters in the novel or the events in the movie were fictional, I would have no hesitation in telling you they were made up. At the same time, I simultaneously know that the emotions I experienced were powerful and moving—*and real*. Anna Karenina and Daenerys Targaryen and the old man who went fishing in the ocean and caught a fish that was too big for him never existed, but what *I* experience as I read or watch their stories *is real*. It brings me in touch with my hopes and fears, it makes me see things in a new way. It reminds me of the potential for horror that lies inside me, and the potential for greatness, too.

Why can't the same be true for religious texts? You may not believe that Jesus was actually crucified and rose from the dead, or that Mohammed directly heard the word of God or that the Hindu god Hanuman lifted up a mountain. But why should that mean those stories cannot inspire you, or move you to be a better human being? The fundamentalists who argue incessantly with each other about the truth-claims of religion tell us that the only way to derive value from those stories is to believe them entirely, or that there can be no value in those stories since they cannot be proven true. But if the stories have resonance and power, does it really matter if they are true? Why put the emphasis on the truth or falsity of the stories, *rather than on what the stories do for us?*

The late University of Cambridge philosopher of science Peter Lipton used to call himself a "religious atheist." One of his central contentions was a theme that has emerged repeatedly in the course of this book—stories, metaphors and symbols are central to the working of the brain, and they are essential to our well-being. Lipton told me that he was *both* a card-carrying rationalist and a religious believer. He said he squared the circle by seeing religious texts as akin to great novels or poems. "Here I am in a synagogue on a Saturday morning and I say the prayers and say all these things to God and engage with God and yet I don't believe God exists," he said. "As I am saying that prayer, I recognize it as being a statement to God. I understand it literally and it has meaning because of the human sentiments it expresses. I am standing saying this prayer that my ancestors said, with feeling and intention, those things are moving to me. What I am saying is, maybe that is enough."

Acknowledgments

Shankar Vedantam

S ince I didn't know very much about podcasting when I launched the *Hidden Brain* podcast in 2015, I took the liberty of educating myself by running lots of experiments. Many of these turned out to be poorly conceived, and were quickly discarded. But others stuck. One of my best inventions is a feature called "The Unsung Hero." It is a short note attached to the credits at the end of each podcast episode, designed to call attention to someone who works in the background, or whose contributions to the episode are implicit rather than explicit. (If the person who paints your house is a "sung hero"—his or her contributions are clear and obvious— the person who invents the ladder used by the house painter is an "unsung hero.") Hosting the *Hidden Brain* podcast and writing this book have helped me realize that once you start noticing them, unsung heroes are legion.

This book has a great many sung and unsung heroes. Bill and I would like to thank our editor, Matt Weiland, who—when not playing soccer hooligan—is wise, reserved and funny. From the first moment we signed on to work with Matt, we knew we had made the right decision. (Matt quickly realized otherwise, but was stuck.) Along the way, he countered our many doubts, false starts and misgivings by keeping us in a state of perpetual hope and positive expectation. In other words, he had mastered the central message of our book before we wrote it. I have great appreciation for my literary agent, Laurie Liss of Sterling Lord Literistic. I treasure her good counsel in all literary matters—actually, scratch that. I treasure her good counsel in *all* matters. Bill would like to say the same about his agent, the irrepressible and irreplaceable Gail Ross of Ross Yoon Agency.

My debt to the hundreds of researchers whose insights and voices and stories fill these pages is immense. Many scholars in these pages allowed me to conduct lengthy interviews for the *Hidden Brain* podcast, for other NPR stories, and for articles I wrote during my time as a reporter and columnist at the *Washington Post*. These include Dan Ariely, Emily Ogden, Ted Kaptchuk, Bruce Moseley, Debu Purohit, Baba Shiv, Americus Reed, Iain McGilchrist, John Deighton (whose paper about the role of seduction in marketing first tipped me off to the story of the Church of Love), Nicholas Hobson, Scott Atran, Annette Gordon-Reed, Andrés Reséndez, Sheldon Solomon, Jeff Greenberg, Tom Psyzczynski, Stephen Cave, Azim Shariff and Daniel Kahneman. Some of the other researchers whose ideas have informed my thinking in this book include Cailin O'Connor, Tali Sharot, Sendhil Mullainathan, Jonah Berger, Seth Stephens-Davidowitz, Kate Darling, Clay Routledge, Lera Boroditsky, Paul Rozin, Andie Tucher, Adam Galinsky, Francesca Gino, Jennifer Bosson, Emily Ogden and Asbjørn Hróbjartsson. The personal narratives in the book that bring scientific ideas to life required the willingness and courage of people to tell their stories. Bill and I are immensely grateful to Joseph Enriquez, whose remarkable story changed the way we think about many fundamental questions. We would also like to thank Ken Blanchard, Tate Chambers, Don Lowry, Jerry Schick, Lt. Kenneth Rexroth, Pete and Hope Troxell, Linda Buonnano and Julie Irwin Zimmerman, Bella De Paulo, Jorge Trevino, Emily Balcetis, Hilary Frooman, and Don Lowry's sons, Tor and Rico.

If I were to list the many colleagues at NPR, the *Washington Post* and the *Philadelphia Inquirer* who have played an important role in shaping my thinking on the themes of this book, I might need an acknowledgements section as long as the book itself. (Listeners of the *Hidden Brain* podcast and readers of my *Washington Post* column, *Department of Human Behavior*, will surely notice many echoes in these pages of ideas I have explored in newspaper and podcast stories.) I am deeply grateful to NPR, which offered me a warm and welcoming home for several years. Among colleagues, I owe special thanks to Tara Boyle for her journalistic instincts, strategic vision and emotional intelligence. Tara knows more about my hidden brain than nearly anyone else. My admiration for her is boundless. Deep thanks also to Kara McGuirk-Allison, who helped me invent *Hidden Brain*, and was a fan and friend in the days before the podcast became a success. I am deeply grateful to the many journalists who have helped me build *Hidden Brain*—their names will be familiar to listeners of the show: Jenny Schmidt; Rhaina Cohen, who produced episodes on the placebo effect and terror management theory that greatly inform the chapters "The Theater of Healing" and "The Grand Delusion"; Parth Shah; Thomas Lu and Laura Kwerel, who produced episodes featuring Azim Shariff and the philosopher Stephen Cave, who play important roles in the chapter "The Grand Delusion." A big shout-out to Jenna Weiss-Berman, Maggie Penman and Max Nesterak, and my old "stopwatch science" sparring partner Dan Pink. These are the best colleagues I have ever known, and among the smartest and nicest people in my life—they make me grateful not just in these pages, but every day. I am deeply thankful to Ira Glass for helping me tell the story of the Church of Love on *This American Life,* and for being the kind of genius who isn't impressed with his own genius. Producer Stephanie Foo, truly a force of nature, might well be the biggest unsung hero of this book—that original radio story might never have happened without her. *Morning Edition* hosts Steve Inskeep, David Green, Rachel Martin and Noel King have welcomed me on their show time and time again, and helped me bring interesting ideas to life with their incisive questions and witty repartee. (Steve, in particular, helped invent what eventually became *Hidden Brain*; I will be forever grateful to him for his collegiality and generous spirit.) Anya Grundmann, Lynette Clemetson, Madhulika Sikka and Anne Gudenkauf—a formidable quartet of brilliant journalists and managers—shaped the creation of *Hidden Brain* over many years. Dozens of others at NPR, the *Washington Post* and the *Philadelphia Inquirer* helped give me the time and space to explore the ideas that fill these pages. A short (and grossly inadequate) list of people includes Adam Zissman, Jarl Mohn, John Lansing, Loren Mayor, Kinsey Wilson, Neal Carruth, Steve Nelson, Kenya Young, Tracy Wahl, Cara Tallo, Dotty Brown, Nils Bruzelius, Steve Holmes, Rob Stein, Demian Perry, Isabel Lara, Bryan Moffett, Brett Robinson, Tanya Blue, Erin Sells, Camille Smiley, Gemma Hooley, Meg Goldthwaite, Michael Lutzky, Adam Cole, Paul Haaga, Camilla Smith, and Howard Woolner. I will always be grateful to Paul Ginsburg, who was the first to suggest I start a podcast: As I've said on the show, he saw something in me that I had not seen myself—and that is the greatest gift one person can give another.

There is an old saying: Behind every podcast host and author is an exhausted family. To Gayatri and Vish, who exemplify Ernest Hemingway's definition of courage—to show grace under pressure—and to my mother, Vatsala, to whom this book is dedicated, thank you. My daughter, Anya, gives me the kind of pride and joy that the Egyptian kings mentioned in these pages could only dream about—she is the kindest, most thoughtful and compassionate person I know. When I grow up, I want to be like her. My wife, Ashwini, makes everything I do possible—I am so grateful for her spine of steel, her brilliant mind and her attentive and open heart.

Notes

Throughout Don Lowry's trial in 1989, there were a slew of newspaper and magazine stories about the Church of Love, as well as feature segments on all the major television networks. Much of the factual information contained in these reports was exaggerated, misinformed or flat-out wrong. (Unsurprisingly, most contemporaneous media accounts focused on the tawdry and titillating aspects of the scam, but as lead prosecutor Tate Chambers said at Don Lowry's trial, "sex is the sizzle that sells the steak.") We've instead drawn upon court documents and interviews with key participants in the scheme, including prosecutors, members and Don Lowry himself. We've also cautiously drawn from a self-published memoir written by Lowry late in his life. It's a one-sided account written by someone with a rather casual relationship to the truth. (At one point, Lowry claims that the television show *The Beverley Hillbillies* was stolen from a pilot he wrote, and that he had given to *Twilight Zone* creator Rod Serling.) The memoir is titled *Mastermind*, which says something about the author's opinion of himself. But despite its reportorial errors and narcissistic excess, it is still an interesting account of one of the strangest cons in American history.

Sigmund Freud's references to the city of Rome are drawn from *Civilization and Its Discontents*. It is worth reading not so much for the specific theories he proposes—so many of which have been rejected—but as a historical document that illuminates the changing way in which experts have conceived of the workings of the mind. (The use of a Freudian metaphor by two science journalists skeptical of Freud is positively Freudian.)

Donald Hoffman's *The Case against Reality: Why Evolution Hid the Truth from Our Eyes* explores how our minds are designed to prioritize "fitness" over facts—it looks at how we attend to things and perceive the world in ways that maximize our odds of survival and reproduction, rather than in ways that maximize truth and accuracy.

The analogy about life on Earth playing out over a 100-yard field came from a wonderful NPR story by Adam Cole titled, "Watch Earth's History Play Out on a Football Field." We highly recommend it—it makes us rethink our place in creation every time we watch it.

The references to Richard Dawkins in this book don't capture the enormous influence he has had on the popular understanding of evolutionary biology. Ironically, to the extent we are challenging Richard Dawkins in these pages, we are channeling . . . Richard Dawkins: In defending reason and rationality against the forces of self-deception in books such as *The God Delusion*, Dawkins seems to have underestimated the power of the ideas he himself has long championed. If you truly accept that human existence is the product of natural selection, then it ought to follow that the many faculties of the mind that produce self-deception (as well as the faculties that produce logic) are the product of natural selection. Looked at this way, our capacity for delusional thinking might not be a bug, but a feature.

1. HOT AIR

Harvey Sacks' essay "Everybody Has to Lie," first published in 1975 in the academic book *The Dimensions of Language Use*, contains the kind of revelations that everyone at first denies (few of us admit to being a serial liar) but later seem so obviously true that they cease to seem like revelations. Information on Robert Feldman's experiment on deception is taken from his delightful book *Liar: The Truth About Lying*. Robert Trivers' book *The Folly of Fools* is essential further reading for those interested in exploring the evolutionary origins of self-deception, as is Ajit Varki and Danny Brower's *Denial*.

The reference to the research on lying by psychologist Bella DePaulo and colleagues can be found in the paper "Lying in Everyday Life." The study on rudeness, "How Incivility Hijacks Performance," was conducted by Christine Porath, Trevor Foulk and Amir Erez. Further details on these studies can be found in the bibliography, as can details about all the studies mentioned in these notes or referenced within the book.

If you didn't catch the original series *Key & Peele* and their skits about the "Anger Translator" Luther, do yourself a favor and track them down on YouTube, where you can also find the performance by Keegan-Michael Key and President Obama at the 2015 White House Correspondents' Dinner.

2. EVERYTHING IS GOING TO BE OK

Anyone interested in the psychology of lying should check out the work of Dan Ariely (and the *Hidden Brain* podcast episode about his work titled "Liar, Liar.") Ariely has long grappled with the human capacity for deception and self-deception, and has found ways to combine a rigorous approach to science with a deeply humane understanding of human nature. We've drawn from a slew of studies pertaining to optimism, most of which are easy to find by scanning the bibliography.

We drew on philosopher and Kant expert Helga Varden's paper, "Kant and Lying to the Murderer at the Door," for our description of Kant's views on deception. For parental lies, we relied heavily on Gail D. Heyman, Diem H. Luu and Kang Lee's "Parenting by Lying" and Penelope Brown's "Everyone Has to Lie in Tzeltal." There is lots of research into the effects of optimism on health, but one good place to begin further reading is the paper by Toshihiko Maruta, Robert Colligan, Michael Malinchoc and Kenneth Offord at the Mayo Clinic titled "Optimists vs Pessimists: Survival Rate Among Medical Patients Over a 30-Year Period," which tracked 839 patients from the 1960s to the 1990s to find that "a pessimistic explanatory style . . . is significantly associated with mortality." "The Comforting Fictions of Dementia Care," a *New Yorker* piece by Larissa MacFarquhar, is a superb exploration of the benevolent deception medical professionals increasingly practice on the elderly and infirm. The story of how the opioid crisis affected Pete Troxell's family can be heard on the *Hidden Brain* episode "The Lazarus Drug."

3. THE THEATER OF HEALING

For Franz Mesmer's story, we drew on the original report written by Benjamin Franklin and his fellow commissioners at the time of their investigation into Mesmer. We've also drawn from Thomas Szasz's *The Myth of Psychotherapy*; Christopher Turner's piece "Mesmeromania, or, the Tale of the Tub" from *Cabinet* magazine, and Claude-Anne Lopez's paper "Franklin and Mesmer: An Encounter" from the *Yale Journal of Biology and Medicine*. University of Virginia scholar Emily Ogden's entertaining history of Franz Mesmer, *Credulity*, also informed our thinking.

Mark Best's "Evaluating Mesmerism, Paris, 1784" contains some illuminating look at the episode in regard to our modern understanding of placebo. And in recent years, the placebo has been the subject of a number of stories in the *New York Times* and other leading publications. We've referenced several of them in the bibliography.

More details about Ted Kaptchuk's studies into the placebo effect, as well as Bruce Moseley's placebo surgery experiments and Emily Ogden's account of Mesmer's rise and fall, can be heard on the *Hidden Brain* podcast episode "All the World's a Stage—Including the Doctor's Office."

4. THE INVISIBLE HAND

The hilarious "designer water" segment from Penn and Teller's *Bullshit* is available on YouTube. Throughout this chapter, we've drawn from various studies conducted by Baba Shiv, Dan Ariely and colleagues, including "Placebo Effects of Marketing Actions, Consumers May Get What They Pay For" and "Marketing Actions Can Modulate Neural Representations of Experienced Pleasantness," which contains the experiment that monitored the way the brain experiences pleasure when drinking wine. Baba Shiv can be heard on the *Hidden Brain* episodes "Forgery" and "How the Brain Tells Real from Fake: From Fine Art to Fine Wine." He also appears in articles written by Shankar for the *Washington Post*.

Joshua Bell's incognito street performance is described beautifully by reporter Gene Weingarten in his *Washington Post* story "Pearls Before Breakfast." Americus Reed can be heard on the *Hidden Brain* episode "I Buy, Therefore I Am: How Brands Become Part of Who We Are."

5. THE HEART HAS ITS REASONS

Joseph's story is the product of many long interviews over the years, both by phone and in person. Shankar's first piece on Joseph, "Jesse's Girl," aired on the *This American Life* episode entitled "The Heart Wants What It Wants" and is available on the show's website. Other versions have aired on the *Hidden Brain* podcast, including in the episode, "Lonely Hearts." At his request, in all the radio pieces, Joseph was identified only by his middle name, Jesse. He graciously allowed us to use his first and last names for this book.

Our understanding of positive illusions relies upon numerous research studies, particularly the work of psychologists Lauren Alloy and Lyn Abramson, and on psychologist Shelly Taylor's book *Positive Illusions* and the academic paper she coauthored with colleague Jonathan Brown, "Illusion and Well-Being."

Dan Marom, Alicia Robb and Orly Sade's paper, "Gender Dynamics in Crowdfunding (Kickstarter)" provided an unusual window into the benefits of self-deception in entrepreneurial success. Their work also appears in a *Hidden Brain* story on NPR's *Morning Edition*.

If you haven't seen Errol Morris's classic *Gates of Heaven*, be sure to do so. It is a remarkable movie that captures the human need for companionship and love.

6. PREDICTIVE REASONING

In addition to the *New York Times* opinion piece "Why You Will Marry the Wrong Person," Alain de Botton has delivered his "lower your expectations" recipe for marital harmony in numerous public appearances, many of which are available in video form on YouTube. We also drew on a large swath of academic research. Among these are "The Benefits of Positive Illusions: Idealization and the Construction of Satisfaction in Close Relationships"; "Inattentive and Contented: Relationship Commitment and Attention to Alternatives"; "Perception and Meta-perceptions of Self and Partner Physical Attractiveness"; "Mirror, Mirror on the Wall: Enhancement in Self-Recognition." The Montclair State University experiment that monitored the role of the medial prefrontal cortex in self-deception was described in the paper "Assessing the Neural Correlates of Self-Enhancement Bias."

The Jerome Bruner experiment that recognized the effect of wishful seeing on rich and poor children was first described in "Value and Need as Organizing Factors in Perception," a 1947 paper he wrote with Cecile Goodman. We've also drawn on a host of papers and experiments by Emily Balcetis, often in tandem with David Dunning. Over the years, the *Hidden Brain* podcast, as well Shankar's eponymous 2010 book, have explored many facets of deception and self-deception (examples being too numerous to enumerate here).

For a good summary of some of the scientific theories about the Miracle of the Sun, read the *Live Science* article "The Lady of Fátima and the Miracle of the Sun" by Benjamin Radford, deputy editor of *Skeptical Inquirer* magazine. Our primary source for the story of William Mumler was Louis Kaplan's *The Strange Case of William Mumler, Spirit Photographer.*

7. SOMEWHERE OVER THE RAINBOW

Leo Festinger's *When Prophecy Fails* is a classic book, remarkable both for its importance—it established the theory of cognitive dissonance—and as a weird piece of history. The events described in *When Prophecy*

Fails are reprised in an excellent 2011 story in *Chicago* magazine, "Apocalypse Oak Park: Dorothy Martin, the Chicagoan Who Predicted the End of the World and Inspired the Theory of Cognitive Dissonance." The details of the Church of Love trial were drawn from court transcripts and detailed interviews with prosecutors, defense attorneys, law enforcement officers, former members of the Church of Love and Don Lowry.

Because we assume that most readers of a book like this are already familiar with the concept of cognitive dissonance, we deliberately avoided a detailed exploration of the concept. But for further reading, check out *Mistakes Were Made (But Not by Me)* by the psychologists Carol Tavris and Elliot Aronson.

8. WALKING THROUGH FIRE

Our understanding of the situation in Bulambika—and Congo in general—relies on various media and human rights reports, but the particulars of the story are drawn mostly from the paper by economists Nathan Nunn and Raul Sanchez de la Sierra, "Why Being Wrong Can Be Right: Magical Warfare Technologies and the Persistence of False Beliefs." The *New York Times* piece "The Most Unconventional Weapon" contains useful information on modern African bulletproofing rituals and the role of magical beliefs among soldiers about to do battle. Diana Preston's *The Boxer Rebellion* offers a Western-centric account of this history. A vastly more detailed account of the events is contained in *The Origins of the Boxer Uprising* by historian Joseph Esherick. Even those not all that interested in the Boxer Rebellion might find it worthwhile to read Mark Twain's essay "To the Person Sitting in Darkness," on the injustices and hypocrisies of Western imperialism.

Statistics on the spending on rituals of the very poor are taken from statistics gathered by the Nobel Prize–winning economists Abhijit V. Banerjee and Esther Duflo and published in their paper, "The Economic Lives of the Very Poor." We've drawn on several studies conducted by Nicholas Hobson and his colleagues, including "When Novel Rituals Lead to Intergroup Bias: Evidence from Economic Games and Neurophysiology" and "The Psychology of Rituals: An Integrative Review and Process-Based Framework." (Hobson has also been featured in a *Hidden Brain* story on NPR's *Morning Edition*.) We've also drawn on a number of studies by anthropologist Dimitris Xygalatas and his colleagues. For anyone interested in his work, check out his captivating account, "Trial by Fire," published in the internet magazine *Aeon*.

9. SOMETHING WORTH DYING FOR

"What Is a Nation?" was first delivered as an 1882 lecture by French historian Ernest Renan. The fact that it continues to be reprinted and discussed is evidence that the question has never been satisfactorily resolved. First published in 1983, political scientist Benedict Anderson's book *Imagined Communities* remains one of the most important and relevant studies of nations and nationalism.

Israeli historian Noah Yuval Harari's book *Sapiens* includes an excellent chapter on the value of the uniquely human capacity for fiction and our penchant for making stuff up. It is a superb book and would make for excellent further reading for anyone interested in the role delusion played in in the early development of societies and the construction of our world.

A lot of the research on the psychology and motivation of ISIS fighters comes from an interview Shankar conducted with Scott Atran. For more reading, take a look at "The Devoted Actor's Will to Fight and the Spiritual Dimension of Human Conflict," a paper written by Scott Atran and colleagues. Atran has discussed the psychology of ISIS at length in his essay "Why ISIS Has the Potential to Be a World-Altering Revolution," available online in *Aeon*, and in a similar piece titled "The Islamic State Revolution" that appeared in *Prism*, the magazine of the U.S. National Defense College. Atran can be heard on the *Hidden Brain* episode "The Psychology of Radicalization: How Terrorist Groups Attract Young Followers."

The quote from Slavoj Žižek was delivered in the Slovene film *Houston, We Have a Problem!*

10. THE GRAND DELUSION

For this chapter, we drew on a number of interviews and a number of books, all of which would make for useful further reading. Ernst Becker's *The Denial of Death*, published in 1973, is a thought-provoking look at how the knowledge of death shapes our lives. The same can be said for *The Worm at the Core*, by psychologists Sheldon Solomon, Jeff Greenberg and Tom Pyszczynski. It is the essential read for anyone interested in terror management theory. Stephen Cave's book *Immortality* is a compelling summation of different theories surrounding humankind's quest to live forever. Besides the books, lengthy interviews Shankar conducted with Cave and Solomon are featured in the *Hidden Brain* podcast episodes "We're All Gonna Die!" and "We're All Going to Live Forever!" Shankar's interviews from his time at the *Washington Post* with Jeff Greenberg and Tom Pyszczynski also came in useful. Jesse Bering's excellent meditation on belief, *The Belief Instinct*, contains a thoughtful examination of the interaction between human psychology and the knowledge of death. The neurologist V. S. Ramachandran's musings on the origins of self-deception can be found in his paper "The Evolutionary Biology of Self-Deception, Laughter, Dreaming and Depression: Some Clues from Anosognosia." His wonderful book *Phantoms in the Brain* has some fascinating insights into the neurological origins of delusion, as does Iain McGilchrist's equally superb *The Master and His Emissary*.

For our discussion of the Egyptian belief in the afterlife, we leaned on *Book of the Dead: Becoming God in Ancient Egypt*, a collection of essays published by the Oriental Institute of the University of Chicago. Thomas Hoving's book *Tutankhamun: The Untold Story* is a well-written account of the greatest archaeological discovery in Egypt, and supplied us with a wealth of detail about Egyptian burial practices.

Azim Shariff's ideas about the "cultural evolution" of religion are explored in detail in Shankar's interview with him on the *Hidden Brain* podcast episode "Creating God."

EPILOGUE

Julie Irwin Zimmerman can be heard on the *Hidden Brain* podcast episode "Screaming Into the Void." Jennifer Whitson and Adam Galinsky's paper in the journal *Science*, "Lacking Control Increases Illusory Pattern Perception," is required reading for those interested in the psychology of false belief and conspiracy theories.

Bibliography

Lauren Alloy and Lyn Abramson, "Judgement of Contingency in Depressed and Nondepressed Students: Sadder but Wiser?" *Journal of Experimental Psychology* 108, no. 4 (1979): 441–485.

Dan Ariely, *The Honest Truth About Dishonesty* (New York: Harper Perennial, 2012).

Jeff Aronson, "Please, Please Me," *The BMJ* 318 (Mar. 13, 1999): 716.

Scott Atran, "The Islamic State Revolution," *Prism*, Oct. 25, 2016.

Scott Atran, "Why ISIS Has the Potential to Be a World-Altering Revolution," *Aeon*, May 21, 2019.

Emily Balcetis et al., "Affective Signals of Threat Increase Perceived Proximity," *Psychological Science* 24, no. 1 (2012): 34–40.

Emily Balcetis et al., "Focused and Fired Up: Narrowed Attention Produces Perceived Proximity and Increases Goal-Relevant Action," *Motivation and Emotion* 38, no. 6 (2014): 815–822.

Emily Balcetis and David Dunning, "See What You Want to See: Motivational Influences on Visual Perception," *Journal of Personality and Social Psychology* 91, no. 4 (2006): 612–625.

Emily Balcetis and David Dunning, "Wishful Seeing: More Desired Objects Are Seen as Closer," *Psychological Science* 21, no. 1 (2010): 147–152.

Emily Balcetis, "Wishful Seeing," *The Psychologist*, Apr. 6, 2019.

Abhijit V. Banerjee and Esther Duflo, "The Economic Lives of the Very Poor," *Journal of Economic Perspectives* 21, no. 1 (2007): 141–168.

Dick Barelds and Pieternel Dijkstra, "Positive Illusions about a Partner's Personality and Relationship Quality," *Journal of Research in Personality* 45 (2011): 37–43.

Rebecca Rego Barry, "Inside the Operating Theater: Early Surgery as Spectacle," *JSTOR Daily*, Dec. 9, 2015.

Andreas Bartels and Semir Zeki, "The Neural Correlates of Maternal and Romantic Love," *NeuroImage* 21 (2003): 1155–1166.

Ernst Becker, *The Denial of Death* (New York: The Free Press, 1973).

Daniel Bergner, "The Most Unconventional Weapon," *New York Times*, Oct. 26, 2003.

Mark Best et al., "Evaluating Mesmerism, Paris, 1784: The Controversy over the Blinded Placebo Controlled Trials Has Not Stopped," *Quality and Safety in Health Care* 12, no. 3 (2003): 232–233.

Matthias Bopp et al., "Health Risk or Resource? Gradual and Independent Association between Self-Rated Health and Mortality Persists Over 30 Years," *PLoS One* 7:e30795 (2012).

Susan Boyce and Alexander Pollatsek, "Identification of Objects in Scenes: The Role of Scene Background in Object Naming," *Journal of Experimental Psychology: Learning, Memory, and Cognition* 18, no. 3 (1992): 531–543.

Penelope Brown, "Everyone Has to Lie in Tzeltal," in *Talking to Adults*, ed. Shoshana Blum-Kulka and Catherine E. Snow (Mahwah, NJ: Lawrence Erlbaum, 2002), 241–275.

Jerome Bruner and Cecile Goodman, "Value and Need as Organizing Factors in Perception," *Journal of Abnormal and Social Psychology* 42, no. 1 (1947): 33–44.

Stephanie Bucklin, "Depressed People See the World More Realistically," *Tonic*, June 22, 2017.

Ken Burns and Dayton Duncan, *The Dust Bowl: An Illustrated History* (San Francisco: Chronicle Books, 2012).

Stephen Cave, *Immortality* (New York: Crown Publishers, 2012).

Sara Chandros Hull et al., "Patients' Attitudes about the use of Placebo Treatments: Telephone Survey," *The BMJ* 347 (2013): f3757.

Leonard A. Cobb et al., "An Evaluation of Internal-Mammary-Artery Ligation by a Double-Blind Technic," *New England Journal of Medicine* 260 (1959): 1115–1118.

Emma Cohen et al., "Rower's High: Nehavioural Synchrony Is Correlated with Elevated Pain Thresholds," *Journal of the Royal Society: Biology Letters* 6 (2010): 106–108.

Mechelle Colombo and John T. Kinder, "Italian as a Language of Communication in Nineteenth-Century Italy and Abroad," *Italica* 89, no. 1 (2012): 109–121.

Richard Dawkins, *The God Delusion* (Boston: Houghton Mifflin Company, 2006).

Alain de Botton, "Why You Will Marry the Wrong Person," *New York Times*, May 28, 2016.

John Deighton and Kent Grayson, "Marketing and Seduction: Building Exchange Relationships by Managing Social Consensus," *Journal of Consumer Research* 21 (Mar. 1995).

Bella DePaulo et al., "Lying in Everyday Life," *Journal of Personality and Social Psychology* 70, no. 5 (1996): 979–995.

Joel Dimsdale, *Survivors, Victims, and Perpetrators: Essays on the Nazi Holocaust* (Baskerville: Hemisphere Publishing, 1951).

Gerald Echterhoff, René Kopietz and E. Tory Higgins, "Adjusting Shared Reality: Communicators' Memory Changes as Their Connection with Their Audience Changes," *Social Cognition* 31, no. 2 (2013): 162–186.

Timothy Egan, *The Worst Hard Time* (Boston: Houghton Mifflin, 2006).

Nicholas Epley and Erin Whitchurch, "Mirror, Mirror on the Wall: Enhancement in Self-Recognition," *Personality and Social Psychology Bulletin* 34, no. 9 (2008): 1159–1170.

Joseph Esherick, *The Origins of the Boxer Uprising* (Berkeley: University of California Press, 1987).

Robert Feldman, *Liar: The Truth about Lying* (New York: Virgin, 2009).

Leo Festinger et al., *When Prophecy Fails* (Minneapolis: University of Minnesota Press, 1956).

Benjamin Franklin et al., "Report of the Commissioners Charged by the King with the Examination of Animal Magnetism," reprinted in the *International Journal of Clinical and Experimental Hypnosis* 50, no. 4 (2002): 332–363.

Sigmund Freud, "Obsessive Actions and Religious Practices," *The Standard Edition of the Complete Psychological Works of Sigmund Freud*, vol. IX (1906–1908): *Jensen's "Gradiva" and Other Works*.

Jane Fruehwirth, "Religion and Depression in Adolescence," *Journal of Political Economy* 127, no. 3 (2019): 1178–1209.

Josh Garret-Davis, "Ghost Dances on the Great Plains," *Guernica*, July 16, 2012.

Aaron Garvey, Frank Germann and Lisa Bolton, "Performance Brand Placebos: How Brands Improve Performance and Consumers Take the Credit," in *Advances in Consumer Research* vol. 43, ed. Kristin Diehl and Carolyn Yoon (Duluth, MN: Association for Consumer Research, 2015), 163–169.

Peter Gay, *The Freud Reader* (New York: W. W. Norton, 1989).

Ángel Gómez, Scott Atran et al., "The Devoted Actor's Will to Fight and the Spiritual Dimension of Human Conflict," *Nature Human Behaviour* 1 (2017): 673–679.

Jochim Hansen et al., "When the Death Makes You Smoke: A Terror Management Perspective on the Effectiveness of Cigarette On-pack Warnings," *Journal of Experimental Social Psychology* 46 (2010): 226–228.

Noah Yuval Harari, *Sapiens* (New York: Harper Collins, 2011).

Gail D. Heyman, Diem H. Luu and Kang Lee, "Parenting by Lying," *Journal of Moral Education* 38, no. 3 (2009): 353–369.

Nicholas M. Hobson et al., "The Psychology of Rituals: An Integrative Review and Process-Based Framework," *Personality and Social Psychology Review* 22, no. 3 (2018): 260–284.

Nicholas M. Hobson et al., "When Novel Rituals Lead to Intergroup Bias: Evidence from Economic Games and Neurophysiology," *Psychological Science* 28, no. 6 (2017): 733–750.

Donald Hoffman, *The Case against Reality: Why Evolution Hid the Truth from Our Eyes* (New York: W. W. Norton, 2019).

Thomas Hoving, *Tutankhamun: The Untold Story* (New York: Cooper Square Press, 2002).

Mathew Hutson, "The Power of Rituals," *Boston Globe*, Aug. 18, 2016.

Louis Kaplan, *The Strange Case of William Mumler, Spirit Photographer* (Minneapolis: University of Minnesota Press, 2008).

Ted Kaptchuk et al., "Placebos without Deception: A Randomized Controlled Trial in Irritable Bowel Syndrome," *PLoS ONE* 5, no. 12 (2010): e15591.

Ted Kaptchuk et al., "Sham Device v Inert Pill: Randomized Controlled Trial of Two Placebo Treatments," *British Medical Journal* 332 (2006): 391–397.

Virginia S. Y. Kwan et al., "Assessing the Neural Correlates of Self-enhancement Bias: A Transcranial Magnetic Stimulation Study," *Experimental Brain Research* 182 (2007): 379–385.

Marin Lang et al., "Effects of Anxiety on Spontaneous Ritualized Behavior," *Current Biology* 25 (2015): 1892–1897.

Irwin Levin and Gary Gaeth, "How Consumers Are Affected by the Framing of Attribute Information Before and After Consuming the Product," *Journal of Consumer Research* 15, no. 3 (1988): 374–378.

Claude-Anne Lopez, "Franklin and Mesmer: An Encounter," *Yale Journal of Biology and Medicine* 66 (1993): 325–331.

Larissa MacFarquhar, "The Comforting Fictions of Dementia Care," *New Yorker*, Oct. 1, 2018.

Spyros Makridakis and Andreas Moleskis, "The Costs and Benefits of Positive Illusions," *Frontiers in Psychology* 6, no. 859 (2015).

Jon Maner et al., "The Implicit Cognition of Relationship Maintenance: Inattention to Attractive Alternatives," *Journal of Experimental Social Psychology* 45 (2009): 174–179.

Sandra Manninen et al., "Social Laughter Triggers Endogenous Opioid Release in Humans," *Journal of Neuroscience* 37, no. 25 (2017): 6125–6131.

Peter Manseau, *The Apparitionists: A Tale of Phantoms, Fraud, Photography and the Man Who Captured Lincoln's Ghost* (New York: Houghton Mifflin Harcourt, 2017).

John De Marchi, *The Immaculate Heart: The True Story of Our Lady of Fatima* (New York: Farrar, Straus and Young, 1952).

Dan Marom, Alicia Robb and Orly Sade, "Gender Dynamics in Crowdfunding (Kickstarter): Evidence on Entrepreneurs, Investors, Deals and Taste-Based Discrimination," *SSRN* (2016), https://papers.ssrn.com/sol3/papers.cfm?abstract_id=2442954.

Toshihiko Maruta et al., "Optimists vs Pessimists: Survival Rate among Medical Patients over a 30-Year Period," *Mayo Clinic Proceedings* 75 (2000): 140–143.

Iain McGilchrist, *The Master and His Emissary* (New Haven: Yale University Press, 2009).

Murray G. Millar and Karen Millar, "Detection of Deception in Familiar and Unfamiliar Persons: The Effects of Information Restriction," *Journal of Nonverbal Behavior* 19 (1995): 69–84.

Rowland Miller, "Inattentive and Contented: Relationship Commitment and Attention to Alternatives," *Journal of Personality and Social Psychology* 73, no. 4 (1997): 758–766.

Whet Moser, "Apocalypse Oak Park: Dorothy Martin, the Chicagoan Who Predicted the End of the World and Inspired the Theory of Cognitive Dissonance," *Chicago*, May 20, 2011.

Sandra L. Murray, John G. Holmes and Dale W. Griffin, "The Benefits of Positive Illusions: Idealization and the Construction of Satisfaction in Close Relationships," *Journal of Personality and Social Psychology* 70, no. 1 (1996): 79–98.

Ara Norenzayan and Ian G. Hansen, "Belief in Supernatural Agents in the Face of Death," *Personality and Social Psychology Bulletin* 32, no. 2 (2006): 174–187.

Paul Novotny et al., "A Pessimistic Explanatory Style Is Prognostic for Poor Lung Cancer Survival," *Journal of Thoracic Oncology* 5, no. 3 (Mar. 2010): 326–332.

Nathan Nunn and Raul Sanchez de la Sierra, "Why Being Wrong Can Be Right: Magical Warfare Technologies and the Persistence of False Beliefs," *American Economic Review Papers and Proceedings* 107, no. 5 (2017): 582–587.

Emily Ogden, *Credulity: A Cultural History of U.S. Mesmerism* (Chicago: University of Chicago Press, 2018).

Elaine Pagels, *Why Religion?* (New York: Harper Collins, 2018).

Marvin Perry and Frederick M. Schweitzer, *Antisemitism: Myth and Hate from Antiquity to the Present* (New York: Palgrave Macmillan, 2002).

Hilke Plassmann et al., "Marketing Actions Can Modulate Neural Representations of Experienced Pleasantness," *Proceedings of the National Academy of Sciences* 105 (2008): 1050–1054.

Robert M. Poole, "How Arlington Cemetery Came to Be," *Smithsonian Magazine*, Nov. 2009.

Christine Porath and Amir Erez, "Does Rudeness Really Matter? The Effects of Rudeness on Task Performance and Helpfulness," *Academy of Management Journal* 50, no. 5 (2007): 1181–1197.

Diana Preston, *The Boxer Rebellion: The Dramatic Story of China's War on Foreigners That Shook the World in the Summer of 1900* (New York: Berkley Books, 1999).

Benjamin Radford, "The Lady of Fátima and the Miracle of the Sun," *Live Science*, May 2, 2013.

V. S. Ramachandran, *A Brief Tour of Human Consciousness* (New York: Pi Press, 2004).

V. S. Ramachandran, "The Evolutionary Biology of Self-Deception, Laughter, Dreaming and Depression: Some Clues from Anosognosia," *Medical Hypotheses* 47 (1996): 347–362.

V. S. Ramachandran and Sandra Blakeslee, *Phantoms in the Brain* (New York: Harper Perennial, 1998).

Geoffrey M. Reed et al., "Realistic Acceptance as a Predictor of Decreased Survival Time in Gay Men with AIDS," *Health Psychology* 13, no. 4 (1994): 299–307.

Research Council of Norway, "World's Oldest Ritual Discovered—Worshipped the Python 70,000 Years Ago," *Science Daily*, Nov. 30, 2006.

Frances Romero, "A Brief History of Unknown Soldiers," *Time*, Nov. 11, 2009.

David Roth and Rick Ingram, "Factors in the Self-Deception Questionnaire: Associations with Depression," *Journal of Personality and Social Psychology* 48, no. 1 (1985): 243–251.

Harvey Sacks, "Everybody Has to Lie," in *Sociocultural Dimensions of Language Use*, ed. Ben G. Blount and Mary Sanches (New York: Academic Press, 1975), 57–80. Reference to this as the first written version of this paper is in "Truth Is, Everyone Lies All the Time," *The Conversation*, May 13, 2012.

Foy Scalf, ed., *Book of the Dead: Becoming God in Ancient Egypt* (Chicago: Oriental Institute of the University of Chicago, 2017).

Azim Shariff and Ara Norenzayan, "Mean Gods Make Good People: Different Views of God Predict Cheating Behavior," *International Journal for the Psychology of Religion* 21 (2011): 85–96.

Azim Shariff and Ara Norenzayan, "God Is Watching You," *Psychological Science* 18, no. 9 (2007): 803–809.

Baba Shiv, Ziv Carmon and Dan Ariely, "Placebo Effects of Marketing Actions: Consumers May Get What They Pay For," *Journal of Marketing Research* 42 (Nov. 2005): 383–393.

Sheldon Solomon, Jeff Greenberg and Tom Pyszczynski, *The Worm at the Core* (New York: Random House, 2015).

Jason Steinhauer, "The Indians' Capital City: Native Histories of Washington D.C.," *Library*, Mar. 27, 2015.

Pamela Stewart and Andrew Strathern, eds., *Ritual* (New York: Routledge, 2010).

Sheryl Gay Stolberg, "Sham Surgery Returns as a Research Tool," *New York Times*, Apr. 25, 1999.

Viren Swami, Lauren Waters and Adrian Furnham, "Perception and Meta-perceptions of Self and Partner Physical Attractiveness," *Personality and Individual Differences* 49 (2010): 811–814.

Thomas Szasz, *The Myth of Psychotherapy: Mental Healing as Religion, Rhetoric, and Repression* (Syracuse, NY: Syracuse University Press, 1978).

Margaret Talbot, "The Placebo Prescription," *New York Times*, Jan. 9, 2000.

Shelley Taylor and David Armor, "Positive Illusions and Coping with Adversity," *Journal of Personality* 64, no. 4 (1996): 873–898.

Shelley Taylor and Jonathan Brown, "Illusion and Well-Being: A Social Psychological Perspective on Mental Health," *Psychological Bulletin* 103, no. 2 (1988): 193–210.

Shelley Taylor, *Positive Illusions* (New York: Basic Books, 1989).

Robert Trivers, *The Folly of Fools: The Logic of Deceit and Self-Deception in Human Life* (New York: Basic Books, 2011).

Christopher Turner, "Mesmeromania, or, the Tale of the Tub," *Cabinet*, Spring 2006.

Eric Vance, *Suggestible You* (Washington: National Geographic, 2016).

Helga Varden, "Kant and Lying to the Murderer at the Door . . . One More Time: Kant's

Legal Philosophy and Lies to Murderers and Nazis," *Journal of Social Philosophy* 41, no. 4 (2010): 403–421.

Ajit Varki and Danny Brower, *Denial: Self-Deception, False Beliefs, and the Origins of the Human Mind* (New York: Twelve, 2013).

Laura Wallace et al., "Does Religion Stave Off the Grave? Religious Affiliation in One's Obituary and Longevity," *Social Psychological and Personality Science* 10, no. 5 (2019): 662–670.

Rachel E. Watson-Jones and Christine Legare, "The Social Functions of Group Rituals," *Current Directions in Psychological Science* 25, no. 1 (2016): 42–46.

Gene Weingarten "Pearls Before Breakfast," *Washington Post*, Apr. 8, 2007.

Alison Wood Brooks et al., "Don't Stop Believing: Rituals Improve Performance by Decreasing Anxiety," *Organizational Behavior and Human Decision Processes* 137 (2016): 71–85.

Honor Whiteman, "Laughter Releases 'Feel Good Hormones' to Promote Social Bonding," *Medical News Today*, Jun. 3, 2017.

Jennifer Whitson and Adam Galinsky, "Lacking Control Increases Illusory Pattern Perception," *Science* 322 (Oct. 3, 2008): 115.

Dimitris Xygalatas et al., "Extreme Rituals Promote Prosociality," *Psychological Science* 20, no. 10 (2012): 1–4.

Dimitris Xygalatas, "Trial by Fire," *Aeon*, https://aeon.co/essays/how-extreme-rituals-forge -intense-social-bonds.

Index